More Than We Imagined

Appreciative Inquiry for Early Childhood
and Everywhere That Matters

Ellen M. Drolette

Published by EDLINKS® Press
PO Box 205
Essex Junction, VT 05453
United States of America
edlinkspress@edlinks.com
ISBN: 978-1-967024-14-8
First Printing, 2025

For Nora Ellen, Zachary Todd, and Evelyn Marie

You are the reason I keep believing in what's possible.

May you always be curious, kind, and full of wonder.

May you always know the power of your voice,

the beauty of your questions,

and the light you bring into the world.

You are and will always be, more than we imagined.

Table of Contents

FOREWORD

If you've ever had the pleasure of sitting in a room with Ellen Drolette, you know her presence feels like an invitation—to reflect, to connect, and to imagine what's possible. She doesn't rush to fix what's "wrong." Instead, she listens for what's strong. And in doing so, she shifts the energy in a way that opens doors, softens defenses, and brings people back to their "why."

That is precisely what this book does, too.

Appreciative Inquiry isn't just a tool, it's a mindset. And in the high-stakes, high-stress world of early childhood education, where so much of the focus is often on deficits, gaps, and what's not working, Ellen's approach is a radical and necessary reframe. She reminds us that meaningful change doesn't always begin with identifying problems. Sometimes it starts by recognizing and building on what's already working, what's already good.

Through stories, reflections, and practical strategies, Ellen offers a roadmap for leaders and educators who are ready to lead with curiosity, courage, and compassion. This book is a gift to anyone working to create more connected, collaborative, and emotionally sustainable early learning environments.

Whether you're a teacher, a director, a coach, or a policymaker, you'll walk away from these pages with tools to not only see your program with new eyes, but to believe more deeply in the people within it.

Ellen's work is rooted in respect. It honors the complexity of early childhood systems, the wisdom of those who care for young children, and the power of asking better questions. Questions that lead us not just toward solutions, but toward each other.

I am grateful for her voice, her vision, and for this contribution to our field. May it spark new conversations, new hope, and new ways forward.

Alyssa Blask Campbell

CEO, Seed and Sew

Author of Tiny Humans, Big Emotions and Big Kids, Bigger Feelings

A New York Times Bestselling Author

"The only person you are destined to become
is the person you decide to be."

-Ralph Waldo Emerson

PREFACE

Is this book for you?

This book offers practical resources and guidance, drawn from my perspective as an early childhood educator, leader, and lifelong learner reflecting on the central role of relationships in our work. It is written for early childhood and elementary educators, administrators, and anyone who aims to apply these concepts to create meaningful change in their lives and communities.

What Is Appreciative Inquiry?

Appreciative Inquiry (AI) is a way of approaching people, challenges, and systems through a lens of strength and potential. Rather than starting with what is broken, AI asks "What is working?" and "What do we want more of?"

That approach fosters substantial growth on personal, professional, and systemic levels. It is not about ignoring problems, but about engaging with them differently and starting from a place of capacity and connection.

From my perspective, Appreciative Inquiry (AI) is no longer just a professional tool. It has become a way of being. It shapes how I coach, lead, listen, and live. Whether I'm teaching, writing, or spending time with family, AI grounds me in what matters most: relationships, reflection, and the belief in possibility, even in the face of challenges.

Appreciative Inquiry calls us to focus on the conditions that allow individuals, teams, and communities to thrive, rather than chasing quick fixes or temporary solutions. It is a strengths-based approach that feels both practical and deeply human.

Using AI doesn't mean sidestepping difficulties. Instead, it means beginning from a place of capacity, connection, and hope. Whether I am supporting educators, writing, or listening to a child, AI reminds me to look for what's important and to help others recognize their own brilliance.

Our shared goal as early childhood educators, parents, and grandparents is to nurture strong social-emotional growth in children and their families. This is work that truly takes a village. Human growth and learning flourish only when social and emotional well-being are prioritized.

Appreciative Inquiry offers us a way to make better choices, choices that strengthen children's lives, support families, and advance our field. Helping children and families reach their full potential requires more than strategies alone; it calls for curiosity, reflection, and a commitment to building on what is already working. Together, we can create environments where everyone has the chance to thrive.

At its heart, Appreciative Inquiry draws on the lived experiences of those who ask better questions, believe deeply in human potential, and embrace the power of strengths-based perspectives. Their influence has shaped both this book and my own life, and I hope their wisdom will spark inspiration in you as well.

The roots of the strengths-based movement can be traced to pioneering scholars and practitioners who reimagined how change happens, not through deficit analysis, but by inquiring into what gives life to individuals, organizations, and communities. From this radical and hopeful perspective, Appreciative Inquiry was born.

Writing this book has been something I have dreamt about for quite some time. Appreciative Inquiry has been a guiding force in my life, even before I had the words for it. Questions like "What's working?", "What are our strengths?", and "How can we improve?" interested me. These questions defined my roles as educator, colleague, and leader.

Appreciative Inquiry's principles resonated with me; it felt like I'd found my place. I found the ideas and practices consistent with my belief that meaningful change stems from curiosity, connection, and the courage to imagine something better.

In this book, I merge my life and learning. It's a reflection of the children, families, educators, and communities who have shaped me along with my family, and it is a celebration of what's possible when we choose to look for the good, even in hard moments.

I hope these pages offer you not only insight but also inspiration: to notice what is working, to amplify strengths, and to reimagine what early childhood education and life can be when we lead with hope.

-Ellen M. Drolette

Chapter One

THE BEGINNING

"Start where you are. Use what you have.
Do what you can."

-Arthur Ashe

I began my career in 1993, not with a grand plan, but with a simple and urgent need: I could not find quality childcare for my own children. What started as a deeply personal frustration became the spark that set the course for my life's work.

In those early days, I was motivated first and foremost by love, wanting the very best for my children. But as I stepped into the field, that motivation quickly expanded. I began to see not only my own family's needs, but also the struggles of countless others searching for care that was safe, nurturing, and truly responsive to children. What started as one mother's search became a calling rooted in advocacy, equity, and the belief that every child deserves the opportunity to thrive.

Over time, my work grew beyond meeting a personal need. It became a commitment to reimagining what quality childcare could look like, to lifting up educators, and to innovating in a field that is too often undervalued but holds immeasurable importance. The journey that began with a closed door, my inability to find the care I needed, has opened countless others: opportunities to lead, to write, to coach, and to be part of a movement dedicated to children, families, and the professionals who care for them.

Today, my own "babies" are raising babies of their own. Watching them grow as parents continues to shape and inspire the story I share, both in my work and in my life. They've always been my biggest cheerleaders in the background, even as I have had to learn a new role: one of quiet support. There are moments when I want to jump in, fix their problems, and wrap everything up like a perfectly tied gift. But they've taught me the power of listening, of giving them space to vent, process, and find their own way, without always unleashing the mama bear in me.

That personal connection to caregiving has never left me. It has simply evolved. As my role shifted from mother to mentor, from advocate to elder, I came to recognize that the same instinct that first drew me to this work, the deep desire to nurture and protect, still shows up in powerful ways. But now, it's not just about offering support; it's about knowing when to hold space instead of stepping in.

Sometimes I feel an overwhelming urge to fix everyone's problems, as if their discomfort is mine to solve. When someone around me is upset, their emotions seem to seep into me, shifting my internal state before I even realize it. Their stress becomes my stress. Their sadness, my weight to carry. I lose track of where their feelings end and mine begin.

Recognizing this pattern hasn't been easy, but it's been essential to my growth. I am learning that empathy does not require emotional absorption, and that caring does not mean carrying it all. As I untangle my own feelings from those around me, I rewrite old patterns, letting go of the need to please, to fix, or to hold pain that was never mine to begin with.

The reflex to step in and make things better comes from a place of care, but it can also leave me exhausted, anxious, and unsure of what I feel. I am striving to overcome my people-pleasing habits.

My epiphany happened more recently than I am willing to admit. My friend Alyssa asked in passing, "How were the holidays with your kids and grandkids?" I replied, "Good, I guess. Everyone seemed to be happy."

I said it casually, as if outward happiness from everyone else meant I had done my job as a parent. She laughed and replied, "If I have ever heard a classic Ellen response, that's it!"

That moment stuck with me. Her gentle humor revealed something deeper: somewhere along the way, I had internalized the idea that visible joy equaled success. That minor exchange nudged me to reflect on a bigger truth.

Over time, I have learned that I can't control others' emotions or choices; I can only take responsibility for myself. Constantly striving to make others happy, I risked neglecting those who mattered most, including myself.

What if I stopped calling myself a "people-pleaser" and instead embraced being a "relationship-oriented thinker"? That shift in perspective changed how I saw myself and how I moved through the world.

This theme shows up often in my work. As an educator, mentor, parent, and grandparent, I have had to develop strategies to manage stress, burnout, and compassion fatigue. Realities that run deep in early childhood education. I have also seen colleagues struggle when families were upset about program closures, sick policies, or late pick-ups at the end of the day.

We all get stuck in patterns. We fill in gaps with assumptions, misread cues, and take on more than we should. Once we see the patterns, we can rewrite them with clarity, boundaries, and intention.

Holding On to Hope While Holding It All Together

In 2018, I published my first book, titled Overcoming Teacher Burnout: Strategies for Change. This book draws on my extensive background in early childhood education. The short stories in my book reflect the personal struggles of a diverse group of educators. Before understanding Appreciative Inquiry, I used reframing and other tactics to deal with field issues.

I shared the strategies I gained over the years as an early childhood educator, from being mindful to taking care of my mental health, as well as having my own young children in my program, discussing my challenges with burnout, being a business owner, working with families, and the details that went into running a childcare program while emphasizing the "how" and "why" in early childhood programs. I concentrated on strategies that have helped me grow. I will share some of those stories here with deeper reflection that looks at growth through the years.

My first book's creation coincided with my earning my Appreciative Inquiry Practitioner certification. I thought I was doing this year-long course because I wanted it to be a tool for elevating my business and realized later that I gained a framework to live my life and the most significant strategy for overcoming burnout.

Nine months after my book was released, we faced a global pandemic, unlike anything most of us had witnessed. COVID-19 turned the world upside down. It touched every aspect of life: health, the economy, daily life, and mental health. After my book had been published, I had some keynote opportunities that were cancelled when the pandemic hit. I was devastated.

The grief was both personal and shared. Hearing the phrase "collective grief" for the first time, I felt a powerful connection to the people in my life experiencing losses. People missed weddings, funerals, graduations and milestones that mark the rhythm of life. We were all navigating different stages of the grief cycle, often without the tools or space to process what was happening. As a country and as a global community, we're still feeling the ripple effects today.

Children returned to classrooms, masked, after months at home. Children as young as two and three wore masks. We are just beginning to understand this period's potential impact on language development, socialization, and emotional security.

Many of us persevered, using the unexpected time on our hands to reframe challenges into strengths-based solutions. Stretching our thinking and embracing new realities as things shifted. People started thinking more creatively, imagining new ways to live, work, and connect. I cleaned my childcare space, organized every closet, and scanned years of photo albums. I had time. Time for reflection: I required time to contemplate my past and future. I had never had ten weeks to pause, reassess, and refresh. That, for me, was the silver lining.

Reimagining What's Possible After the Pause

Naturally, many unanticipated effects resulted from the pandemic.

Let's concentrate, though, on significant worldwide benefits stemming from the pandemic.

For the first time, the government classified early childhood educators, caregivers, and childcare programs as essential workers. Families highlighted the incompatibility of working from home and being the childcare. Families experienced stress.

Eventually, the programs, policies, and field earned respect. For example, the importance of sick policies and the need to stay home when ill. Businesses of all sizes realized they couldn't ignore a child's illness with Tylenol. This realization for families trying to balance work and family presented insurmountable challenges for parents of toddlers and preschoolers.

During the COVID-19 pandemic, Vermont's government recognized the urgent need to support early childhood education; not just to keep programs afloat, but to protect families and the future of our

workforce. They understood the long-term consequences of widespread program closures: families left without care, educators out of work, and a national crisis deepening.

The early childhood field was weakened by years of underfunding, making it vulnerable to the pandemic. Programs were already closing because of the inability to offer livable wages, and many operated on razor-thin margins. Several weeks of closure risked permanent shutdown. The price of health and safety materials needed to reopen would have overstretched our budget.

Vermont answered the request. During and after the shutdown, our state provided vital financial aid and resources. This unwavering commitment underscores the critical importance of early childhood education investment.

We've made dramatic progress in digital skills. FaceTime and Zoom were essential for staying in touch with colleagues, family, and students during missed holidays, birthdays, and graduations. Technology eliminated the distance barrier.

This moment let us refine our Appreciative Inquiry. Showing empathy and creativity, we addressed families' multifaceted challenges. Joy was a key outcome. We celebrated small wins, whether it was stepping outside for a walk or sharing a laugh on video chat.

Another key step was the acceptance of reinvention. New ways of celebrating, reinterpreting traditions, and using technology for deeper human connection developed.

These efforts serve as inspiring models for how we can promote the essential role of early childhood education and advocate for its continued growth.

Making Meaning of What We Do and Why It Matters

Problem-solving and Appreciative Inquiry have different focuses; one on assets, the other on problems. This allows for personal and professional growth by transforming challenges into opportunities.

Appreciative Inquiry experienced substantial growth during the 1980s and 90s. In this period, the 4-D model (this will be covered later on) transitioned to the 5-D model. Appreciative Inquiry also gained global recognition through five international conferences that brought together researchers, practitioners, and change makers. In 2010, Champlain College in Burlington, Vermont, opened the David L. Cooperrider Center for Appreciative Inquiry at the Robert P. Stiller School of Business, the first academic center in the world dedicated to the advancement of Appreciative Inquiry. This became possible thanks to a transformative $10 million gift from Robert and Christine Stiller in 2012. We'll return to Robert Stiller's story and the impact AI has had on his business a bit later.

From Knowing to Becoming

My introduction to Appreciative Inquiry happened during a leadership institute. We addressed different aspects of leadership every month. We dedicated a month to Appreciative Inquiry (AI).

With a local school superintendent serving as the expert that month, participants learned ways to use the AI framework's capabilities and how the school used this with its stakeholders. This is where it all began for me. Even with this introduction to AI being spotty. I remained curious.

Later, I had a meeting with Dr. Laurel Bongiorno, the former Dean of Education and Human Studies at Champlain College. With a shared history in early childhood education, she was familiar with my perspectives on growth, learning, and relationships. She believed Appreciative Inquiry was the right next step for my lifelong learning journey and introduced me to the Appreciative Inquiry Practitioner

Certification offered in my hometown at Champlain College in Vermont.

As a small business owner still finding my footing, the cost felt significant, and the year-long commitment was no small thing. I had to ask myself whether this would truly benefit my professional growth. But something in me knew it was worth the risk. I took a leap of faith, hoping to gain one more tool for my tool belt, and what I received went far beyond that.

Our Vermont course began on a stunning autumn day. As I stepped into a meeting room at Champlain College, I was welcomed by some of the most joyful, grounded, and inspiring instructors I have ever met: Prue Sullivan, Joep C. de Jong, and Dr. Lindsey Godwin. Their energy, wisdom, and authenticity set the tone for what would become one of the most transformative learning experiences of my career, maybe even my life!

From the moment I arrived, I knew I'd found my community.

Despite my anxiety, the group's open and vulnerable nature was comforting.

I was seated at a table where four other unfamiliar faces were already present. A woman from the Midwest held a leadership position at a school that practiced positive education. A kind pastor was present; a woman who spoke softly had moved with her husband to assume the leadership of a church. I recognized a familiar face among my colleagues in Vermont, someone from Shelburne Farms. His work focused on a farm-to-school initiative, collaborating with early childhood education programs and various schools to facilitate its implementation. Present at the event was a librarian who worked at an extensive city library system on the West Coast. A few who joined us had traveled from afar to be part of the event.

Meeting and connecting with pioneering figures in Appreciative Inquiry has been both humbling and inspiring. What struck me most about leaders like Dr. David Cooperrider, Jacqueline Kelm, Robin Stratton-Berkessel, Dr. Jacqueline Stavros, and Dr. Cheri Torres was not only their brilliance, but also their humility. Each of them took the principles of AI and found a way to live them out in their own unique context, transforming practice into purpose.

Dr. David Cooperrider, the originator of Appreciative Inquiry, showed the world that change rooted in possibility and strengths could spark transformation at every level, from organizations to global initiatives. Jacqueline Kelm translated AI into the language of everyday life, making it accessible through her work on personal and practical applications. Robin Stratton-Berkessel brought AI into conversations and storytelling, helping groups and individuals unlock creativity and connection through her focus on design and facilitation. Dr. Jacqueline Stavros, alongside Dr. Cheri Torres, co-created Conversations Worth Having, showing us how the questions we ask every day can shape culture, collaboration, and leadership in powerful ways.

Each of these pioneers found their niche by weaving AI into their own teaching, coaching, writing, or leadership. Together, they have expanded the reach of Appreciative Inquiry. Co-creating a body of work that is both practical and deeply human, and that continues to ripple out across the world.

I dedicated the initial months of my Appreciative Inquiry practice to intensive study. To gain a deeper understanding of Appreciative Inquiry and its practical applications, I devoted considerable time to researching online articles and watching many YouTube videos that showcased various real-world examples of its implementation. I wanted to understand the method and even the philosophy behind it.

Two key books, "The Joy of Appreciative Living" by Jacki Kelm and "Conversations Worth Having" by Jackie Stavros and Cheri Torres, shaped my outlook. The powerful connection between Appreciative Inquiry and positive psychology became apparent as I read its pages. I learned from these readings that emphasizing strengths, potential, and productive discussions leads to lasting life and career improvements. I was so passionate about this discovery that I started using it daily.

The stories in Conversations Worth Having made me reflect deeply on how I handle tricky conversations with families in my program and with peers. One of the biggest lessons I took away was the realization that I am not responsible for how people respond. For years, I carried the weight of other people's reactions on my shoulders. If a family member left upset, or a colleague seemed frustrated after a conversation, I would replay every word in my head, wondering what I could have done differently, what I should have said, or where I might have gone wrong.

What I have come to understand is that we each step into conversations carrying our own perspectives, assumptions, and histories. A parent may listen through the filter of past experiences with schools or authority. A colleague may respond out of the weight of their day rather than the content of our exchange. Our words are never received in isolation. They are heard and shaped by all that someone brings with them.

There was one moment that stands out. A parent was trying to understand her child's behavior challenges both at home and at child care. I had gone into the meeting prepared, calm, and ready to listen. Still, she reacted with anger, and my old instinct kicked in: that pit in my stomach, that urge to fix it, to smooth it over, to somehow carry the burden of her feelings. But then I remembered, I can't control how she responds. What I can do is stay present, acknowledge her perspective, and respond with curiosity instead of defensiveness.

That shift was powerful. Instead of leaving the conversation drained and second-guessing myself, I walked away knowing I had shown upwith empathy and clarity. The parent still needed time to process, and that was okay. The responsibility for her response did not rest with me. Releasing that pressure allowed me to be more authentic in my conversations.

I am still learning. We all are, but I see tricky conversations less as minefields and more as opportunities. If I approach them with openness, honesty, and curiosity, I create space for connection and trust, even if the outcome isn't immediate. That has been freeing.

As I absorbed the ideas from these powerful books, I saw how the principles of Appreciative Inquiry weren't just professional tools; they were deeply personal. They gave language to something I had always felt: that relationships thrive not through control or fixing, but through curiosity, connection, and shared strengths. This perspective helped me examine my own habits, especially my tendency to seek harmony at all costs. I came to realize that my need to please others often masked a deeper desire for peace and belonging. However, I've learned that peace doesn't come from trying to control others' feelings.

From Jackie Kelm's The Joy of Appreciative Living (Kelm, 2014), I learned that joy isn't something we sit around waiting for. It's something we choose to notice, nurture, and grow. At first, that idea felt almost too simple, but it changed the way I moved through my days. I began paying attention to the little sparks of joy that were already present: the sound of children laughing in the classroom, the way the morning light spilled through the window, a kind word exchanged with a family. The more I noticed, the more I realized that joy multiplies when we tend to it. It is not about waiting for everything to be perfect; it is about choosing to see and celebrate the goodness that is already here. That change not only made me feel better, but it also transformed my approach to interactions, connections, and my job.

Insights in Practice

**AI-Inspired
Questions**

How can I find possibility instead of limitation when I am facing challenges?

What sparks of joy have I already noticed today?

**Reflective
Exercise**

For one week, write down three small moments of joy each day. They can be as simple as a smile, a kind word, or the warmth of morning light. At the end of the week, reread your list. What patterns do you notice?

**Practice
Tip**

In your next tricky conversation, pause before responding. Remind yourself: "I am responsible for how I show up, not for how others respond." Then ask one curious, open-ended question.

Chapter Two

WHAT WE BELIEVE SHAPES WHAT WE DO

"WHAT WE CHOOSE TO NOTICE AND ASK ABOUT IN OUR
CLASSROOMS AND OUR WORLD SHAPES WHAT GROWS. WHEN WE
FOCUS ON STRENGTHS, SUCCESSES, AND POSSIBILITIES, WE
CREATE SPACE FOR MEANINGFUL LEARNING
AND LASTING CHANGE."

-Ellen Drolette

Appreciative Inquiry isn't just something I studied and applied;
it's something I began to live into. The principles weren't just
academic concepts I memorized in a classroom; they emerged
from real-life moments, relationships, and reflections that shaped my
work and who I am. Long before I had the official language of
Appreciative Inquiry, I was already stumbling into these truths: that
words matter, that questions open doors, and that the stories we tell
can either limit or liberate us.

As I deepened my practice, I saw how these principles, developed by
Dr. David Cooperrider and his colleagues, offered more than just a
framework for organizational change. Hope, possibility, connection,
and courage defined their perspective on the world. In Appreciative
Inquiry (AI), the Emergent Principles refer to a second wave of
principles that were articulated after the original five core principles.
These new principles show a shift in how we understand AI's function
in complex systems, particularly in varied real-world scenarios.

In this chapter, I want to share the stories that taught me what
these principles mean, not just in theory, but in lived experience.
You'll see how they showed up in unexpected places: in classrooms
and communities, in heartache and healing, in decisions made with

clarity and courage. I hope that as you read, you'll recognize some of your own story, too.

Words Create Worlds: The Construction of Meaning (The Constructionist Principle)

My childcare program began in 1993 with the goal of doing things the "right" way; I had a lot of passion and drive, even though I did not have much experience with kids. I leaned on what I had seen or believed to be best practice: walls splashed in bold primary colors, shelves packed with plastic toys, and daily craft projects children could bring home to impress their families. In my mind, these choices reflected quality. I wrongly thought parents wanted a structured academic education focused on literacy, numeracy, and basic concepts, and my role was to deliver this.

Looking back now, I understand how much of that early belief system was constructed, not out of ill intent, but out of inherited expectations, unexamined assumptions, and the dominant cultural messages of the time. I had yet to learn what the Constructionist Principle of Appreciative Inquiry would later reveal to me: that words create worlds, and that the stories we tell about learning, about quality, about ourselves, shape what becomes possible.

The shift began when I enrolled in college-level coursework, starting with Child Growth and Development, taught by Dr. Robin Ploof. She had both academic credentials and practical experience running her own early childhood program. One visit to her classroom disrupted everything I thought I knew. Her space was quiet, designed with care, and filled not with overstimulation, but with children's art, photos, and writing. The walls weren't just decorated; they were documenting learning. Children's voices were present, and their ideas were visible.

Robin introduced play not as something extra, but as the foundation of early learning. This was a radical departure from my checklist-style view of early childhood. I began questioning long-held assumptions. I thought about the handprint turkeys I'd once sent home and wondered, "Whose voice is really present here, mine or the child's?"

That's when things changed. Slowly, I moved from a product-focused mindset to a process-oriented one. I listened to children, families, and colleagues. Their language shaped mine. My understanding of what mattered most in early learning deepened. I paid closer attention to how environments felt, not just how they looked. I wanted to create an environment in my program with soft lighting, uncluttered materials, and spaces where children's agency and creativity were on full display.

My practice evolved. Nature walks with field notebooks became a way to nurture observation and curiosity. Reading Stone Soup turned into a tradition of community-building and cooking together. On Valentine's Day, we used my grandmother's china for a "fancy tea party," sparking conversations about kindness and friendship. These weren't just activities; they were rituals that reflected what we valued. They told stories. They created culture.

The Constructionist Principle became real to me, not through theory, but through experience. Every assumption challenged, every tradition I reimagined, was part of constructing a new reality for children, families, and myself. I understood that my program hadn't started with a blank slate; it had started with a story. I had the power, along with others, to reshape it.

What we say, what we assume, what we prioritize, it all matters. Since reality never remains still. It is built moment by moment through our conversations, our language, and our willingness to reflect. Early childhood education is, when all is said and done, a living system. It grows through connection, through what we are willing to question, and through the stories we choose to live into together.

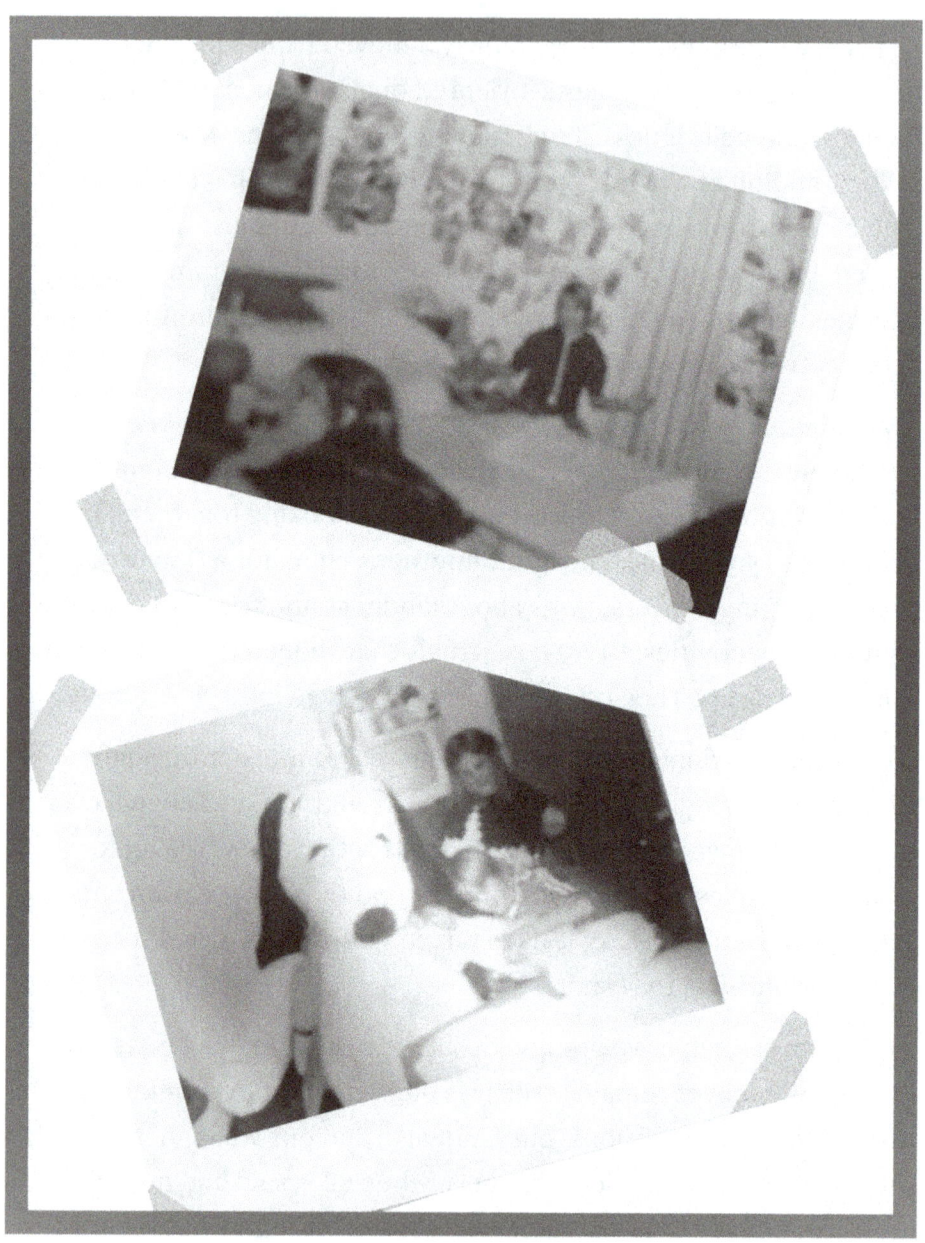

The Questions That Changed the Story
(Simultaneity)

I was in fourth grade when my brother Joseph was badly burned. He was in seventh grade; our sister Leigh was a high school sophomore. Joseph had always been a curious, hands-on kind of kid. The kind who enjoyed figuring things out through trial and error. One late summer he got rid of the tomato worms devouring our garden by dropping them into a plastic bucket of gasoline and setting it on fire.

At the time, my parents were with neighbors, my sister was out on our back deck, and I was walking home from a friend's house, lugging my dolls and doll trunk. I remember reaching the corner before our house and seeing flashing lights, an ambulance, and police cars. I dropped everything and ran home as fast as I could toward our raised ranch home. When I threw open the front door and stood in the foyer, I saw my mother cradling Joseph's head at the bottom of the stairs. He was screaming in pain. I could not see his legs. I did not know exactly what had happened, only that it was serious. As a nine year old, I created a narrative based on what I was hearing from adults, visiting in the hospital, the narrative was based on the little information I had.

I began to put more pieces together. Joseph had tried to stomp out the fire, but his corduroys caught on fire, and the flames wrapped around his legs. He remembered to stop, drop, and roll. A neighbor had shouted for help, and my parents came running. He was rushed to the hospital with second- and third-degree burns that would keep him there for weeks.

The next few months were blurry. My parents spent long days at the hospital, applying cocoa butter to his healing skin, helping him move his legs again. The smell of cocoa butter still brings me back to that time. Leigh became my unofficial guardian, mapping out bus routes, managing my schedule and making my meals. She was fifteen years old.

As a child, I did not know how to process the swirl of emotions. There was fear, yes, but also jealousy. Joseph's room was filled with balloons and stuffed animals. Everyone's attention was focused on him. I remember telling my parents, "He gets so much attention because he's so dumb." Looking back, I cringe at those words, but I understand where they came from. I was nine, and my world had just changed.

Years later, in my late twenties, I saw a psychologist during a period of deep depression. She asked if any major events from my childhood had shaped me. At first, I thought my childhood was pretty amazing. I told her about Joseph's accident. I recounted it the way I had always remembered it, through the lens of a fourth grader, full of emotion and fragments.

Then she asked a question that stopped me cold: "Do you think your sister or your parents would tell the story the same way?"

I remember staring at her. In my head, I thought, What do you mean? We were all there.

But we were not. Not exactly. We were each living inside our own version of the event, shaped by our roles, our emotions, and what we could understand.

That one question did something I did not expect: it rewired my thinking. That is the Simultaneity Principle, that the moment we ask a meaningful question, transformation begins. It is not the answer that changes us, it is the act of asking, of wondering, that opens the door.

More recently, I talked to Leigh and Joseph about that day. Leigh had heard Joseph screaming and looked over the deck railing to tell him to stop yelling. That is when she saw he was on fire. She never told my parents at the moment she saw him on fire. She still does not know why. But she carried guilt for years. At fifteen, she had to grow up fast, becoming both sister and caretaker. Joseph's perspective obviously was very different as well as he dealt with a lot of physical pain, he still managed to be an annoying middle school brother through it all.

As we shared our versions of that day, a new understanding formed. My story had always been framed by confusion, envy and resentment. But now I could see my brother's pain, my mom and dad's fear, my sister's quiet strength. We all lived the same event, but the meaning we made from it was different.

That's the power of a single, well-placed question. It does not just invite reflection; it reshapes the lens entirely. We live in the stories we tell ourselves. And sometimes, the only way to rewrite them is to ask for something new.

The Praxis and the Power of Imagining Success (Anticipatory Principle)

I have always needed a goal, something that gives me focus, keeps me anchored. But for most of my life, I kept those goals to myself. I'd dive in quietly, just in case I failed. If no one knew, no one would be disappointed, not even me. It was true for running, writing my first book, finishing my undergraduate degree, even submitting a proposal to speak at the World Forum for Early Care and Education.

But something changed when I took the Praxis. The Praxis is a multi sectioned test that teachers need to pass to earn their teaching license.

If you've ever had a complicated relationship with tests or with math, you'll understand. I had told myself for years that I wasn't a "math person." I failed algebra twice. Grew up in a system that taught one way, and if you did not learn that way, you were just... stuck. That belief followed me into adulthood. I even panicked during the CPR tests. I had labeled myself as a "bad test-taker" and was further crippled by the anxiety of math combined with tests.

Still, I wanted to become a Vermont state-licensed early childhood educator. And that meant facing the Praxis, a set of reading, writing, and math tests.

I felt okay about the reading and writing parts. But the math? Even looking at a practice question made my heart race. Variables, polynomials, exponents. I did not even speak that language.

I had to remind myself that this content could not be learned quickly and had to focus on learning the ins and outs of Algebra and Geometry. I ordered books. I studied. I took practice tests. I reminded myself that failing wasn't a verdict; it was just information. I also reminded myself that lots of people fail their first time.

My cousin Vinny, a high school math teacher, jumped in to help. We Zoomed. He used virtual whiteboards to walk me through problems. He made it feel less like math and more like translation: "Here's what this question is actually asking."

Still, I was afraid. But here's the shift.

I did not let that fear shape the outcome. This was months of work. While it seems simplified, this mindset shift and narrative took months of work.

I started to visualize passing. I imagined getting my results. I pictured getting the results and texting Vinny, "I did it." It felt awkward at first, this kind of future-visioning was new to me, but I kept doing it.

That's the heart of the Anticipatory Principle, we move in the direction of the future we imagine. Not the one we fear. Not that one someone else mapped out for us. The one we choose to see.

The first time I took the test, I passed the reading and writing portion, but failed the math.

Old me might've stopped there, let the failure reinforce the story I'd carried for years. But this time, I did not flinch. I rescheduled right away. I practiced more. I visualized again. And the second time? I looked at the pieces that did not make sense still and reviewed them. Finally, I passed.

That test wasn't just about math. It was about reclaiming something I thought I had to live without, confidence, agency, possibility.

And it did not stop there.

When I prepared for my first big keynote, standing in front of hundreds of people in Manhattan, Kansas, I used the same approach. I made a playlist of music to calm my nerves. I walked around the space. I chatted with people beforehand to feel grounded. And when the nerves crept in, I whispered to myself: You belong here. You earned this. I pictured myself walking off that stage proud of what I shared, proud of who I was.

The Anticipatory Principle teaches us that positive images of the future shape how we act in the present. And now I know it's true. Because once I let go of the old narrative, the one where I had to hide until I was perfect, I started showing up–honestly. And the future I pictured started showing up, too.

Building Possibility: A Strengths-Based Approach to Change (Positive Principle)

Years ago, I took on a part-time role through a federal grant to support a group of Somali and Nepalese women as they worked toward becoming licensed family child care providers. From day one, we knew the road would be hard. Language barriers, cultural transitions, systemic red tape, all of it stacked against us. But I also knew this: if we focused only on what was broken, we'd never move forward.

I made a choice. I would lead with strength.

These women had already lived through incredible hardship, years spent in refugee camps, raising children without consistent resources or support. But they had also taught in those camps. They knew how to make learning happen with mud puddles instead of water tables, with scraps of fabric instead of parachutes. They did not need to be taught how to care for children, they needed a system that recognized their knowledge and helped translate it into licensure requirements.

That meant getting creative.

We used visuals and simple language supported by interpreters. We explored child development through sensory play, storytelling, and hands-on materials.

They made Oobleck. They created story stones. They crafted homemade books. I brought them into my program so they could observe how we played, co-regulated, talked with children, and built systems that supported safety and growth. I built documentation tools that mirrored what I used myself, like daily checklists, routines, and fire drills, because I knew they worked.

I did not sugarcoat the challenges. But I also did not center them. I asked "What do these women bring?" and "How can I amplify that?"

That's what the Positive Principle in Appreciative Inquiry is all about. It reminds us that positive emotions and strengths-based questions lead to positive change. It's not toxic positivity or blind optimism, it's a choice to anchor in what's possible rather than what's missing.

We started small. They completed homework. They returned with questions. They began to see the connection between talking with their babies and building their brains. They learned that play wasn't a distraction, it was the foundation. Some went on to earn their Child Development Associate credentials. One woman has operated her own family child care home for years. The ripple effect is real: their children are growing up with caregivers who understand not just how to nurture, but why it matters so deeply in the first five years.

At meetings with funders and licensing partners, I could have shown up frustrated by the slow system, the cultural blind spots, the forms that made no sense. And sometimes, yes, that frustration surfaced. But I knew the greater impact would come from showing what was working, inviting stakeholders into home visits, letting them witness firsthand the joy, the commitment, the transformation.

Because when you ask What's possible here? instead of What's wrong here? the answers are completely different. One leads to judgment. The other leads to momentum.

And that's the power of the Positive Principle: when you choose to focus on success, strengths, and hope, you generate energy that propels people forward. You don't ignore reality; you shape it.

Rewriting the Finish Line
(Poetic Principle)

In 2007, I set out to run the Vermont City Marathon, not the relay, not a half, but the full 26.2 miles. It wasn't a spontaneous decision. I had run each leg of the relay before, volunteered at the kids' race, even served on the race committee. I knew the course, the heat, the heartbreak, and the glory. Still, part of me did not feel like a "real runner." Imposter syndrome told me I did not look the part, did not train the part, and that I did not belong at the start line.

But I had something else, a pull toward proving something to myself. I talked my best friend Terry into training with me. We bought the book Running Within, which wasn't your typical running manual. It focused on mental preparation, mantras, visualization, and treating the race like a spiritual journey. One quote stayed with me: "You are good enough. You deserve the best. Act as if this were true."

So I did. I visualized the finish line. I pictured my kids running toward me, the crowd, the sound of cowbells, the feeling of crossing into something bigger than pain or pride. I started writing mantras and tucking them into my pocket for training runs. I whispered to myself on icy hills, "I love hills." I chanted with frozen feet in spring puddles, "We are warriors." I treated every mile like an act of belief.

But belief isn't linear.

One day, a month before the race, I had to complete a solo 16-mile run. Terry couldn't join me, and I panicked. Halfway in, I had a full-blown meltdown (probably more like a panic attack), crying, doubting, unable to breathe. I called my husband, Todd, certain I was not completing that training run.

I approached his truck ready to jump in the passenger side and head home and cry some more. He instead grabbed his bike from his truck and said, "We're finishing this together." While my worst run ever mentally. I was the most sore physically than I had ever been.

The next week, I changed everything I did. I did not just train my body, I trained my narrative. I meditated, journaled, visualized each segment of the race, including the infamous hill on Battery Street. I imagined my kids at the finish, my name being called, the sun on my face. That week also marked Terry's return. I was determined to not let this "long run" be the outcome of the actual marathon day.

The Poetic Principle of Appreciative Inquiry says human systems are like open books, we get to choose what we study, what we focus on, what stories we tell. That marathon wasn't about proving anything to anyone else. It was about choosing a different story.

The day of the race, Missy, my other best friend gave me a note or quote for each leg of the run. Every mile marker became more than distance; it became meaning. I tucked those quotes in my running belt, right next to my gels. The hill that scared me? I smiled as I ran up it. "I love hills." "We are warriors."

Around mile 20, Terry's knee gave out. We slowed. We shuffled. And right on cue, Todd showed up on his bike again, just like he had during that painful 16-miler. He rode beside us, mile after mile, snapping photos at every marker.

When we finally turned into Waterfront Park, a race volunteer was dismantling the finish line banner. My cousin Jim stopped him. "Wait," he said. "They're still coming."

And we did.

My kids ran toward me as I had imagined.

That moment, the finish line, the hugs, the signs, the smiles, wasn't luck or coincidence. It was a story I had written months before, one I had believed in when doubt tried to rewrite the ending.

For years, my inner voice had said, You're not an athlete. You don't belong here. But I had decided otherwise. I had focused on the miles I did walk, shuffle, and jog, the strength I did have, the finish I could see before it ever arrived. And that choice made all the difference.

The Poetic Principle reminds us: what we notice, we nurture. The stories we tell ourselves become the lives we lead. And when we choose to focus on meaning, purpose, and hope, even in the hard moments, we create space for possibility to bloom.

That's not just a race story. That's an early childhood story. It's a human story. We all carry stories that try to define us. But we have the power to rewrite them.

One mile. One mantra. One moment at a time.

Positive questions create positive energy and progress, as the Positive Principle teaches. A shift towards success, strengths, and hope fosters creativity, resilience, and collaboration; problem-solving alone is less effective.

+ What's working well right now?

+ What are you most proud of today?

+ What gives you hope in this situation?

+ When have you seen your team at its best?

+ What strengths are showing up in this challenge?

+ What's one bright spot you can build on?

+ Who has been a helper or encourager for you lately?

+ What recent success can we learn from?

+ What's possible if we focus on what's working?

+ What small step would feel good to try next?

"Positive questions lead to positive change."

Emergent Principles

Appreciative Inquiry's Emergent Principles are a development surpassing its original five core principles. AI's development within complex organizations and communities, highlighted the need for expanded guiding principles to enhance the existing framework. While based on AI fundamentals, these newer principles stress the significance of total participation, ingrained values, and true engagement.

Throughout my experiences, I have frequently mentioned Dr. Lindsey Godwin, Professor of Management and Academic Director of the Cooperrider Center for Appreciative Inquiry at Champlain College, a major contributor to these newer principles.

With her colleagues, Dr. Godwin documented and named the developing trends among global AI practitioners using the approach more inclusively and collaboratively. The global rise of AI, particularly in education, community development, healthcare, and organizational leadership, saw practitioners such as Diana Whitney, Jacqueline Stavros, and Marge Schiller contribute insights and case studies that shaped the principles of Wholeness, Enactment, and Free Choice.

These emergent principles were not authored by a single individual, but surfaced through a collaborative and reflective process within the AI practitioner community. They were documented and formalized in part through the 2015 Appreciative Inquiry Handbook (3rd Edition) by Cooperrider, Whitney, and Stavros, and expanded upon in the work of faculty and researchers at the Cooperrider Center for Appreciative Inquiry. (Cooperrider & Stavros, 2015, #)

The emergent principles reflect AI's own iterative, reflective nature. Just as AI encourages organizations to learn and grow, the field of AI itself has grown by listening to what works in practice and adapting to new insights.

Wholeness Principle

The Wholeness Principle brings out the best in people and organizations by pooling the group's knowledge and expertise to generate new opportunities. By pooling their knowledge and expertise, stakeholders stimulate creativity and build collective capacity. "Inclusivity builds collective capacity."

I learned decisions were being made for our industry without those that do the job at the tables. Small programs rarely had representation at the table. Even with seats available, daytime meetings excluded Family Child Care (FCC) teachers who lacked substitute access. Feeling the weight of that and having access to a substitute, I started to be the person at the table to represent FCC. Having your voice heard at a table and letting your expertise shape solutions is unparalleled.

One group that I spent many years involved in was the Vermont Early Childhood Advocacy Alliance Steering Committee. The Vermont Early Childhood Advocacy Alliance is a statewide coalition of early childhood professionals and providers, parents, and employers working together to improve public policies affecting young children from birth to age eight on health, safety, food security, economic security, and early care and education issues. The representation ranged from those who worked with food insecurity, child care centers, family child care, parent-child centers, and parents and businesses. This incredible group would set the legislative agenda based on the immediate needs of children and families. We had lobbyists and those able to give testimony in place. Most often, these were populations that were rarely heard from. Our legislators were transparent in telling the committee that they did not want to hear about the obstacles from lobbyists or organizations; they wanted to hear from those experiencing the hardships in their own words.

The wholeness principle shows that systems are greater than the sum of their parts, meaning that the interaction between the parts creates something more significant than the individual components alone. As individual elements, such as cogs and gears, combine within a system, their dynamic relationships and interactions create something far more significant. In this powerful, purposeful machine, each gear plays its part.

This metaphor reminds us that no part functions in isolation. For a system to thrive, whether it's a classroom, a workplace, or a community, it needs connection and interdependence among its components. Each "cog" gains significance through collaboration, as their combined effort creates the momentum necessary for the system to achieve its goals.

The principle encourages us to value relationships, recognize interconnections, and foster synergy, enabling the entire system to operate effectively.

Enactment Principle

To make a change, we must "be the change we want to see." Embodying the change we wish to see helps create a living model or prototype of our ideal future. "Acting as if is self-fulfilling."

The Enactment Principle emphasizes the importance of engaging in the desired change, rather than delaying its implementation until some perceived ideal future point. People embody desired values in their daily lives and envision outcomes, thus weaving them into the essence of their being and experiences.

At the Snelling Early Childhood Leadership Institute, we engaged in "consultancy groups." This process allowed small groups of peers to support one another by offering thoughtful perspectives and problem-solving strategies around real-life professional challenges. The structure was intentional: one person presented a dilemma, while others assumed roles such as note-taker, timekeeper, or thoughtful respondent. The goal was to help the presenter think more deeply, gain clarity, and leave with new ideas or potential next steps.

While the format encouraged reflection and collaboration, something about it felt at odds with the Appreciative Inquiry (AI) work I was doing. In our AI class, we had been exploring how powerful it is to ask life-giving questions. Questions that don't just solve problems but open up possibility. When I reflected on the consultancy format through that lens, I noticed how easily the process could fall into problem-fixing mode. It often centered on what wasn't working rather than what strengths could be built upon or what desired future could be imagined.

In true "possibilitizer" fashion, Dr. Godwin encouraged me to bring what I was learning from Appreciative Inquiry to rethink the consultancy model. Could this trusted structure be transformed into something more aligned with appreciative principles? Could we design a process that still held space for real challenges but approached them through the lens of hope, capacity, and vision?

What followed was an experiment in reframing: keeping the supportive elements of consultancy intact, defined roles, focused time, active listening, but shifting the tone and the questions. Instead of diving into what's broken, we began with what's working. Instead of only offering advice, we asked generative questions that helped the presenter clarify what they wanted more of. And perhaps most importantly, we made sure the process left the presenter feeling energized rather than overwhelmed.

The Appreciative Consultancy model grew from that reimagining. Like the original, it works best in small groups of two to five people. But before diving in, each person agrees to a specific role and to hold space from a strengths-based stance. The result? A reflective and empowering conversation that honors both the real and the possible.

1. Step one involves stating what the challenge is and rate it on a scale of 1-10.

2. Step two is a simple reframe lab. Reframe your challenge or problem into a statement of what you want to see accomplished or achieved. A recurring observation in my large-group process experiment was that participants facing interpersonal conflict frequently stalled in step two, unclear about their goals. The person would take some time to think about the reframe.

3. Step three involves the speaker discussing their reframed perspective and the desired outcomes. The speaker articulates their wanted emotions. What are you hoping to see? What are you hoping to learn today? To provide their group with an accurate image of their reframe, they must provide every detail possible. This may be hard; sometimes, presenting them with questions such as What is the positive opposite of what you are experiencing?

4. In step 4, note-takers should listen (keep comments on your notes) and not talk. The presenter has a 15-minute time limit to explain steps 1 through 3. The rest of the group might require clarification or have additional questions. These come in step five.

5. Step 5, When the speaker is done, the note taker and other group members can use this opportunity to ask questions about the feelings or share images, metaphors, or reflections they have about what they heard. Use the questions below as a guide to gathering more information if needed. Remember that you are not fixing their problem. You are being curious and asking questions.

6. In step 6, the group takes some stillness and quiet time to mull over their thoughts. What resonates in your stillness? Make a mental note. I know people want to skip this part, but don't. Become comfortable in the discomfort of being still with your thoughts.

7. In step 7, everyone takes time to "dream" and discuss possibilities. Think big. Use the details given and make a plan. They may sound like, "I wonder what would happen if..." or "I am curious if you have....".

8. In Step 8, reflect and journal. What has been discovered? What have you learned?

9. Check in with the presenter. How are they feeling on a scale of 1-10 (One being the worst and ten being the best? Has it increased from the number they gave at the beginning? At the end of the consultancy, reflect as a group.

See Appendices for template

Questions

+ What would your day look like if I could hand you a magic wand?

+ What do you love about this work?

+ What do you see as possibilities?

+ Tell me about a challenging time when you felt proud at work.

+ Have you seen someone you admire do it in a way you like?

+ How have you asked for help?

+ What drew you in when you first went into this line of work?

+ What does a great day look like and feel like?

+ When have you seen me at my best?

+ When have you had a challenging moment and been resilient?

The Enactment Principle reminds us that meaningful change comes alive when we actively practice the values and possibilities we hope to see, rather than waiting for the perfect conditions. By reimagining the traditional consultancy format through an appreciative lens, we transform problem-solving into an experience of collective possibility-making. Each step, from reframing challenges to sitting in reflective stillness to dreaming aloud invites participants to live out the core tenets of AI in real time. It's not just about resolving an issue; it's about embodying curiosity, hope, and shared vision. In this way, the consultancy group becomes more than a meeting, it becomes a microcosm of an organization that enacts its aspirations now, in every conversation and every courageous question asked.

Narrative Principle

Stories are transformative; we live into the narratives we construct and tell ourselves.

Narratives are funny things. The stories we tell ourselves, often without realizing, shape how we perceive others, how we interpret events, and how we respond in relationships. These internal narratives are built from a mix of personal experience, cultural context, and the meaning we construct both independently and in collaboration with others. Because stories possess transformative power, they can clarify reality or distort it.

Everyone can relate to this: you call or text a close friend or family member. Usually, they reply right away. But this time... nothing. An hour passes. Then several. The longer the silence, the more elaborate your mental story becomes. Are they upset with me? Did I do something wrong? Your mind, desperate for resolution, begins to fill in the blanks with assumptions. After a full day of uncertainty and emotional churn, the phone rings. Your friend, cheerful and unaware of the storm in your head, says, "Sorry! I couldn't find my charger and then I was skiing in the mountains all day with no cell service."

This everyday moment reveals something profound: our internal narratives, especially in moments of uncertainty, can quickly veer into fiction. These imagined stories are influenced not only by our lived experiences but also by unspoken fears, implicit biases, and sometimes unreliable interpretations. In relationships, whether personal or professional—these assumptions shape our behavior.

They can erode trust, fuel misunderstanding, or lead us to act based on emotion rather than truth.

The narrative principle reminds us to pause and examine the stories we tell ourselves. Are they grounded in fact, or are they projections of fear or doubt? In doing so, we make space for curiosity, for clearer communication, and for connection rooted in empathy rather than assumption.

These constructed and co-constructed stories shape our identities, relationships, and perspectives. One example would be an educator who constructs a negative self-perception based on just one challenging experience, telling themselves a story of being "not enough." Been there. In such cases, this can become a self-fulfilling prophecy, thus creating a cycle that limits both.

When combined with their potential for achieving success, their confidence levels are significant factors to consider. In contrast, if we shift the narrative to highlight resilience, growth, and learning, it can empower them to embrace challenges and, more importantly, to thrive in the face of adversity. Recognizing the transformative power of narratives, we can examine and reshape our personal stories, fostering individual growth, deepening mutual understanding, and promoting positive change within ourselves and our wider communities.

Free Choice Principle

People are more committed to positive change when they have the freedom and space to choose how, what, and when they contribute. "Freedom of Choice Empowers"

Freedom of choice affects an individual's sense of autonomy and self-determination. The ability of individuals to exercise their own free will in decision-making processes is critical in fostering a deep understanding of personal empowerment, enhancing their self-esteem and overall well-being. This system allows individuals to align their lives with what they value, need, and desire, thus resulting in greater control over their lives and what those lives produce.

I saw this principle come to life in my involvement with both the Life is Good Playmaker Project and the World Forum Foundation for Early Childhood Education. These experiences weren't part of a planned career trajectory. They were choices I leaned into, sometimes with fear, sometimes with uncertainty, but always with a sense that I had the freedom to say yes to something bigger than myself.

When I joined the Life is Good Playmakers, I did not fully understand how deeply it would shape my personal and professional lens. I chose to step into that community, and with it came new connections, playful rituals, and an unshakable belief in the healing power of optimism. Likewise, when I applied to become a Global Leader through the World Forum Foundation, I did not wait until I "felt ready." I chose to apply anyway. That one decision opened doors to friendships and learning experiences around the globe and conversations that shifted how I understand leadership, equity, and shared humanity.

Each choice required risk and each required me to take responsibility for the outcomes. Sometimes that meant stretching my comfort zone or acknowledging areas where I still needed to grow. But in doing so, I developed confidence not just in my skills, but in my ability to navigate challenges and move forward with integrity.

That's the beauty of the Freedom of Choice Principle: it fuels creativity, resilience, and intrinsic motivation. When people feel they have agency over their lives, they show up differently. They persist longer, think more expansively, and contribute with greater energy and commitment. Choice isn't just about options. it's about ownership.

By encouraging choice in early childhood settings, we cultivate communities that thrive through innovation, well-being, and purpose.

Problem-solving builds resilience and fosters personal growth through learning from successes and failures.

The freedom to choose one's path and make independent decisions contributes to a strong sense of self-worth and personal value. This principle can create an environment where creativity and innovation can thrive.

Human choice sparks imagination, prompting active exploration of uncharted territories and possibilities. Promoting diverse perspectives and solutions has a positive effect on communities, leading to more inclusive and effective outcomes.

Awareness Principle

The Awareness Principle in Appreciative Inquiry teaches us that in order to cultivate meaningful conversations and strong relationships, we must be aware of the unspoken assumptions and biases that influence our thoughts, interactions, and decisions. When we look at what's beneath the surface, our expectations, narratives, and patterns, we create space for intentionality and growth.

This idea is central to my story. For much of my past school experience, I struggled, often labeled as shy, distracted, or disengaged. What I lacked was a learning environment that recognized my strengths, understood my needs, or even considered that multiple learning paths might exist.

Instead, I encountered a narrow view of intelligence and success, where compliance and correctness mattered more than connection and curiosity. Those messages became a part of my internal landscape. I feared math, avoided tests, and developed a narrative that I wasn't good at certain things. The standardized test bubbles were filled in randomly, not from rebellion, but because of being overwhelmed. That moment, quiet but defining, was where my self-fulfilling prophecy began.

Later, during high school, I enrolled in an ecology course, one of the most academically rigorous outside of math. I intended to drop it, convinced I wouldn't succeed. But my teacher saw something different. He called a meeting, expressed his confidence in me, and promised support. That belief, the simple act of someone expecting more, changed everything. I stayed in the class, worked hard, and succeeded. That experience was a turning point. It showed me how expectations, positive or negative, can shape reality.

This idea is known as the Pygmalion Effect, first studied by Rosenthal and Jacobson in the 1960s. Their research showed that when teachers held high expectations, students performed better, even when those expectations were unfounded. Decades of follow-up studies have confirmed the impact of adult perception on a child's development. The language we use, the stories we tell, and the assumptions we carry all influence what a child becomes.

These patterns still show up in early childhood education today. Many educators rely on outdated behaviorist models that overlook individual strengths and rely on extrinsic control like reward charts, rigid consequences, and deficit-focused language. These approaches often cannot meet the needs of neurodivergent children or those with trauma histories, sensory differences, or learning variations. Worse, they can lead to exclusion, reinforcing cycles of shame and missed opportunity.

I once spoke with a director about a young child in her program who was struggling with dysregulation and had spat. The director shared how triggering and unhygienic the behavior felt. I validated her discomfort and then offered another lens: What might this child be communicating through that behavior? Upon further reflection, it turned out the child had become frustrated while trying to put on his shoes. Stress, not discipline, caused his spitting. What if, instead of punishing the behavior, the teacher had acknowledged the emotion?

"Wow, I can see you're really working hard and feeling frustrated. I get it. Putting on boots frustrates me sometimes too. Want some help?"

By approaching the moment with curiosity and empathy, rather than control, we shift from managing behavior to understanding the child's experience.

This aligns with what we now know from brain science. During moments of meltdown, the amygdala takes over the part of the brain responsible for survival responses. Dr. Daniel Goleman coined the term "amygdala hijack" to describe this phenomenon. In these moments, reasoning isn't possible. Support must begin with safety and regulation, not redirection or lecture. Later, when the child is calm, we can reflect together:

"You were so frustrated this morning. What could we try next time? Deep breaths? Asking for help?"

This kind of awareness, of both brain and behavior, allows educators to design responsive, respectful environments where children feel seen, supported, and capable.

A strengths-based lens helps us uncover each child's unique ways of learning, feeling, and engaging with the world.

My colleague Alyssa Blask Campbell, co-author of Tiny Humans, Big Emotions and Big Kids, Bigger Feelings, offers practical tools for understanding how sensory needs influence children's behavior and emotional regulation. She shares personal stories, like how her older son prefers quiet, low-stimulation spaces, so much so that he left his own birthday party to find a quiet room. In contrast, her younger child thrives in high-energy environments, waving at strangers and seeking connection everywhere. Understanding these differences isn't about labels; it's about awareness. When adults see children for who they are, we can plan with intention, not just reaction.

This also applies to adults. The strengths-based approach (SBA) helps teachers reframe their own thinking, reflect on their practices, and support children from a place of possibility. Open-ended questions and reflective dialogue aren't just for kids; they help educators understand families, build trusting partnerships, and uncover professional insights.

Whether in family conferences, team meetings, or interviews, asking strengths-based questions surfaces potential; it brings forward capabilities that might otherwise remain hidden.

The Awareness Principle reminds us that transformation doesn't begin with changing children; it begins with examining our own lenses. The Pygmalion effect and self-fulfilling prophecy show us that our assumptions shape outcomes. When we expect greatness, we create conditions for growth. When we assume deficits, we unknowingly build barriers.

By raising awareness of our own biases, listening with curiosity, and acting with intention, we create cultures where everyone; children, families, and educators have the chance to thrive.

Insights in Practice

AI-Inspired Questions

What am I paying attention to today — problems or possibilities?

What is one strength (in myself, my team, or my family) that I can amplify right now?

Reflective Exercise

Attention Audit: At the end of your day, jot down three moments when you noticed yourself focusing on what wasn't working. Then rewrite each one into an appreciative question. For example:

Instead of: *"Why aren't children listening?"*

Try: *"When do children listen well, and what makes those moments possible?"*

Practice Tip

In your next staff or family meeting, introduce a simple Appreciative Inquiry prompt:

"Tell me about a time this week when you felt proud of how you handled a challenge."

Watch how the energy shifts when the focus is on strengths rather than shortcomings.

Chapter Three

CURIOSITY AS A CATALYST

"POSITIVE QUESTIONS SHOULD ENCOURAGE PARTIES TO THINK
ABOUT AND TUNE IN TO DIFFERENT PERSPECTIVES. THEY
STIMULATE THE IMAGINATION, INVITE PERSPECTIVE-TAKING, AND
ENCOURAGE COMPASSION AND EMPATHY"

-Whitney et al., 2022

I paid little attention to the word "question" prior to learning what an integral piece it is to this practice.

Inquire is another word for question, but not all questions work the same way. Closed questions usually lead to short answers like yes or no, which can limit a child's thinking. Open-ended questions, often beginning with "what?", "how?", or "why?" invite children to expand on their ideas, share feelings, and make connections. For children, this builds language, confidence, and problem-solving skills. For us as educators, choosing open-ended questions shifts our practice too. They help us listen more deeply, discover children's perspectives, and create richer learning moments."

The questions' answers tell the story. "We want human responses rich in feeling and meaning instead of just data. They are effective and appeal to people, not job titles. Stories are good. They invite parties to participate actively and visualize as a group. Stories engage those involved, build relationships, and make discovery a collective process." (Richards, 2012)

How does a person know what kind of question to ask? In the publication, The Art of a Powerful Question, the authors believe that there are factors that can help you develop powerful questions.

A powerful question generates curiosity in the listener. Some examples: What are your hopes and dreams for your child this school year and beyond? If this school year is a booming success for your child, what would that look like to you? Are there any areas where your child could grow or be challenged further? What areas present opportunities for your child's growth and challenges?

I learned to ask different questions, and that was one of the most powerful shifts I experienced through Appreciative Inquiry. Instead of jumping to solutions or focusing on what's wrong, I began asking things like, "What's working here?" or "When have you felt most energized in your role?" These aren't just better questions; they open up possibilities, spark reflection, and honor the wisdom in the room. Whether I'm speaking with educators, children, or community members, I have seen how the right question can light up someone's face or reframe a challenge. It's not about having the answer; it's about holding space for discovery. When we ask with wonder, we create room for creativity, and forward movement. And that's where the magic happens.

See Appendix A for sample questions.

Bringing Heart, and Insight Into Daily Work
Triple R Framework ™ (TRF)

To help design effective learning experiences for young children and adults in early childhood education, I developed the strengths-based Triple R Framework (TRF). Whether used for professional development, team meetings, leadership decisions or lesson planning, the method centers on the well-being, identity, and growth of educators and the children they serve.

Throughout the book, you will see where I have integrated the TRF. The TRF's core is built upon three interconnected components: Relevance, Relationship, and Reflection.

The Triple R Framework

Relevance	Relationship	Reflection
Connecting learning to what matters	Safe space, trust, voice and choice	Invite insight and meaning, not just information

Together, these pillars help shift professional development, social work, teaching, leading and daily practice away from compliance-driven routines toward engaging, sustaining experiences that mirror the best practices we use with children. When applied, this model strengthens adult learning communities, deepens classroom interactions, and builds the emotional resilience essential in any human-centered field.

Relevance is Rooted in Reality

What matters most?

We ensure that everything we do addresses the immediate needs of educators, teams, and children. It can also apply to other areas like advocacy. When training sessions, coaching conversations, lesson plans, and team meetings address the real questions and daily challenges educators face in their classrooms, with families, and within their broader communities, the work becomes meaningful and motivating instead of feeling like just another requirement.

Educators feel appreciated and understood when professional development addresses their daily realities, such as managing challenging behaviors, collaborating with families, accommodating diverse learners, and teamwork. Relevance shows up in designing routines, projects, and activities that reflect children's current interests and developmental goals.

For leaders and coaches, staying relevant means collaborating with staff on solutions using real-world examples, and involving educators in planning and professional development. Whether planning a team meeting, assigning a leadership role, or preparing a training, grounding it in reality ensures it feels authentic, timely, and useful.

By weaving relevance into every layer, like classroom activity, individual growth, team collaboration, and leadership development. We create spaces where educators are more likely to engage deeply, apply new ideas, and sustain meaningful change.

Relationship: Co-Regulation and Community

In high-quality early childhood settings, strong and genuine relationships are vital for both children and caregivers. A foundation of trust, safety, and shared responsibility allows educators to show up, take risks in their practice, and grow together.

Prioritizing relationships means creating spaces where people feel seen, heard, and valued. Leaders and facilitators can model co-regulation and community by opening meetings with mood check-ins, celebrating each other's wins, and sharing leadership roles so everyone has a voice. In coaching and mentorship, relationship-centered practice means listening with curiosity, offering gentle feedback, and walking alongside educators as partners rather than supervisors.

Building relationships at all levels lessens burnout, promotes trust, and cultivates a shared sense of purpose. When educators experience empathy, support, and meaningful connection to colleagues and leaders, they're more prepared and motivated to extend the same relational care to children and families.

These are questions you can use when exploring relationship building. These questions can be tailored for use with whomever you are working with.

Where do you feel most seen and supported in your current work environment? What helps you build trust with the people you work with? How do you know when a relationship at work is strong and authentic? When have you felt safe enough to take a risk in your practice? What made that possible? How do you listen with curiosity in conversations with children, families, or coworkers? How does your team create space for joy and connection during the day?

Use these questions to explore your work relationships and identify what strengthens trust, inclusion, and shared goals. These tools cultivate a culture of valuing every voice and relationship within team meetings, coaching, and self-reflection, thus promoting success in early childhood settings. Posing these questions creates an environment conducive to substantial, sustained change, moving beyond a superficial check-in.

Reflection: Integration and Identity

Through reflection, educators connect their daily work with whom they are as professionals and people. It transforms routine tasks into intentional practice and creates space for self-awareness and connection to purpose. When educators have time and encouragement to process their daily experiences and reconnect with their core values and teaching philosophy, they build a strong sense of identity, a vital ingredient for resilience and sustainability in early childhood education.

Embedding reflection into your practice means asking, "How does this connect to my work and who I aspire to be as an educator? "and "How will I apply this tomorrow? "Staff meetings infused with reflection shift from information dumps to spaces for meaning-making, feedback, and curiosity about how new ideas fit into daily practice.

Lesson planning can integrate reflection by aligning activities with children's strengths, interests, and the teacher's vision. Small habits like quiet journaling, team check-outs, or sharing moments of impact help staff connect daily actions to bigger goals and remind them they are active, evolving professionals whose insights shape the program's culture.

Strengthening Our Voice with the Triple R Framework

Using the TRF as a guide for your advocacy offers a stable, strengths-based approach to the difficulties of early childhood education and community life, promoting purpose and clarity. We should consider: Is this relevant to the needs of our educators, children, and families? Can this build authentic connections and trust? Was there enough space for reflection, learning, and growth in response to this? Replace passive compliance and silence with curiosity and compassion in your company culture.

Grounding your beliefs and actions in the TRF aligns your vision with what matters, advocating for thriving educators, nurturing resilient children, and strengthening communities built on equity, human connection, and shared responsibility for change.

The TRF creates spaces that do more than check a box; they lift educators up, encourage and honor the human side of teaching and learning.

Take a moment to think about your own team spaces: Do they invite people to pause, share, and grow together, or do they drain energy? A fading smile is worth noticing, because when we reflect on what is working, we uncover what's possible.

TRF templates are shared in Appendix B.

Insights in Practice

AI-Inspired Questions

When was the last time I asked a question that truly opened up new thinking for someone?

What would change if, instead of asking "What's wrong?" I asked "What's possible?"

Reflective Exercise

Question Swap: Take a challenge you're facing right now and write down the first question that comes to mind (for example: "Why aren't my staff engaged?"). Now, reframe it into an appreciative question ("When do my staff seem most engaged, and what makes those moments possible?"). Notice how the reframed question shifts your mindset.

Practice Tip

In your next staff meeting, family conference, or team discussion, lead with one open-ended appreciative question such as:

"What's something that went well this week, and how can we build on it?"

"When have you felt most connected to your work recently?"

These kinds of questions not only invite richer stories but also build trust and collective problem-solving.

Chapter Four

PRIORITIES WITH A PURPOSE

"CHOOSING WHAT MATTERS ISN'T ALWAYS LOUD OR OBVIOUS.
SOMETIMES, IT'S THE QUIET DECISION TO
STAY ALIGNED WITH YOUR VALUES, ESPECIALLY
WHEN IT'S HARD."

-Whitney et al., 2022

I have been part of groups where one or more people will take a problem-solving stance to figure out what and why something is not working. The mindset defaults to blame, addressing problems only to uncover more. It highlights weaknesses.

I have known leaders who have moved through life in this way. Deficit-based thinking captivates those who follow leaders. I used to think that this was leadership, identifying problems. We would spend meetings focusing on how people misunderstood early childhood education, blaming individuals, and constantly trying to solve an unsolvable problem. I call this push-and-pull game "Us vs. Them."

Adversarial thinking frequently assumes one's approach is the only valid one. In a 2019 Psychology Today article, Arash Emamzadeh offers two theories regarding us versus them. One psychological theory suggests that when we perceive our group as being in direct competition with another, especially over limited resources, we are likely to experience opposition toward members of that group. The other theory focuses on identity and self-esteem, unrelated to competition. Emamzadeh, in his article, says, "One reason for this is that our self-esteem comes partly from our group membership. We need to feel good about our group and feel good about ourselves. This can apply to any type of group identity." (Emamzadeh, 2019)

Dr. Smitha Bhandri of WebMD highlights the risks of divisive "us vs. them" thinking and provides valuable guidance on mitigating its negative impact. "If you've ever been met with a tough challenge or conflict, you may have felt an 'us against them' mentality. Whatever the source of the stress, it causes you to become defensive. You need to build yourself up by identifying ways you're better than what you're up against. This can lead to a deep-down bias against others. But it doesn't have to be that way. You can overcome the "us against them" mentality and retrain your brain to approach social situations and conflict in a more positive way." (Bhandri, 2024)

Cultivating positivity and abandoning the "us versus them" mentality can improve your social skills and conflict resolution. To understand our community, we need to recognize the multifaceted and nuanced connections that connect us, going beyond simple categorizations. Identify similarities. When you meet new people, find common ground, shared backgrounds, viewpoints, or interests to build rapport. Warmth and empathy facilitate stronger connections. This mindset shift doesn't mean ignoring diverse perspectives. It means honoring them while building bridges through shared values.

Boosting your self-awareness is vital. Observe your inner world: notice how your thoughts, assumptions, and actions affect not only yourself but those around you. Ingrained biases can distort social interactions, so it's essential to recognize them and develop strategies to counter their effects. Doing so creates more inclusive, respectful, and equitable environments.

Bridging the Gap Between Assumption and Understanding

An "us versus them" attitude in early childhood education divides educators from administrators, families from teachers, and programs from policymakers. These divides hinder the very collaboration we need to move forward. When educators are excluded from decision-making, it leads to resentment, disengagement, and resistance to change. When families feel dismissed or feel unheard, it erodes their trust. And when policymakers overlook the insights of those working with young children, the entire field of ECE suffers. This mindset diminishes the value of early learning expertise and creates inefficient and unsustainable silos.

Us vs. Them

Shared Goals
Nurturing children's development
Creating safe, inclusive environments
Building strong, respectful relationships
Preparing children for lifelong learning
Supporting families as partners
Improving program quality and equity
Sustaining joyful, connected classrooms and communities

Us	Them
Teachers	Admin
Veteran Educators	Newer Staff
Full-time	Part-time
Lead Teachers	Assistants
"Easy" Kids	"Challenging" Kids
Neurotypical	Neurodivergent
Compliant	Disruptive
Verbal	Nonverbal Learners
Dominant Culture	Marginalized C
Native English	Multilingual learners
Traditional Gender Roles	Expansive Identities
Public	Private
Center	Home-Based
State Local	Local Decision-Makers
Educators	Policymakers(
Academic	Play-Based Philosophies
Educator	Advocate

Shared Goals

Progress in early childhood education isn't possible without collaboration. It's built through connection, shared purpose, and mutual respect. By fostering open communication, embracing diverse perspectives, and honoring the essential role each person plays in a child's early development, we can shift from a fragmented approach to a more unified, collaborative model.

The good news? The dynamics within our own programs, our microcosms, are within our control.

Real-world examples and concrete strategies improve human collaboration in the face of pandemic impacts and systemic inequalities. Here are some ways to begin.

Start by co-creating shared goals, such as a child's learning and well-being. During a preschool open house, families may be asked to share a single hope for their child's upcoming year. Educators display these aspirations in the classroom and reinforce the partnership between educators and families during family-teacher conferences.

Use proactive, positive communication, especially at the beginning of the school year. For example: A teacher sends "Just Because" postcards home noting something the child did well that week ("Leila helped a friend zip their coat today, so thoughtful!"). These low-stakes, strength-based notes build trust before any concerns need to be addressed.

Focus the discussions on a child's abilities and successes, not just their shortcomings. To illustrate, instead of saying, "Jordan is wiggly and does not listen during circle time," a teacher might say, "Jordan shows a lot of energy and curiosity. We're working on how he can recognize what his body needs before circle so he can focus."

Respect the cultural insights families share and try to understand their viewpoints. This looks like an early learning program creating "culture books" by inviting families to contribute photos, recipes, or traditions. Teachers keep these books in the classroom library and revisit them throughout the year, promoting inclusion and pride.

Understand that the school environment can intimidate or feel judgmental for certain families. During a conversation about a possible developmental delay, the educator validates the family's expertise by saying, "You know your child best. What have you noticed at home?" This invites collaboration and avoids a top-down dynamic.

Communication That Builds and Mends Relationships

Employ diverse communication methods; a teacher uses a weekly text-based check-in with one question families can respond to, like: "What's something your child has enjoyed at home this week?" This creates reciprocal sharing and builds insight.

If you make a mistake, admit it and show how you'll fix it. For example, following a team meeting where a family felt unheard, the director stated, "We failed to understand your point of view, and I apologize for that. Let's meet again to include your perspective."

These small acts of accountability ripple outward. They're not just about repairing one relationship. They model the integrity and responsiveness that build trust. And they point to a larger truth: lasting change often begins in everyday moments.

That's at the heart of the ongoing human rights conversation. How individuals, through intentional action and reflection, can drive meaningful, sustainable change.

A key question raised in the ongoing human rights discussion is how individuals can drive meaningful, lasting change.

For me, reading articles about grieving, coping, and living with intention has become an unexpected source of hope. These reflections remind me that meaningful change doesn't always come from sweeping policies or global movements. Sometimes it begins right here, in the ways we show up, listen, and lead.

We should all reflect: What is within my power to change today? How can I create small, meaningful shifts within the spaces I occupy? While staying informed about current events is important, protecting our mental health is equally essential.

This isn't about overlooking the injustice or minimizing the damage done; let's be clear. We can foster courage, compassion, and clarity by nurturing awareness and well-being. Focusing on strengths and Appreciative Inquiry doesn't equate to ignoring reality. These tools empower us to overcome it. Throughout history, human suffering and systemic injustice have left their mark on communities and influenced our shared narrative.

Protecting Our Hearts in a Hurting World

There's no escaping the concrete nature of early childhood education policy. National decisions about healthcare, funding, immigration, and civil rights show up in our classrooms every day. We see them in the stories families carry, in children's emotional landscapes, and in the questions that are far too big for their age. When injustice is formalized or praised at the top, it sends a message of non-belonging to vulnerable groups.

This "us vs. them" mentality isn't theoretical. It takes root in the ways people are included or excluded, protected or punished, lifted or torn down.

Policies enacted during the Trump administration harmed diversity, equity, and inclusion (DEI) across education, healthcare, and public service. These shifts harmed differently abled individuals, BIPOC communities, LGBTQIA+ people, women, and others who already experience systemic barriers. Justice and humanity suffered a devastating setback, and in our work with children and families, the effects were personal and immediate. Educators found themselves not only supporting children's growth, but helping families navigate fear, uncertainty, and loss of rights or protections.

So, how do we move forward when all we want to do is hide?

I spoke with my mom. She's 83, wise, warm, and heartbroken by what she sees unfolding in our country. She spends time doom-scrolling, absorbing headlines and commentary that blur fact, opinion, and fiction. The weight of it all has made her physically sick. Her tears spill not only from grief, but from the ache of seeing compassion, justice, and human dignity disregarded.

As she named her fears, I thought of a friend who had stepped away from social media to protect their mental health. I suggested my mom consider doing the same, maybe scroll past certain articles, or take a break altogether. I know that feeling: the heaviness of helplessness, when the world feels too big, too broken, and too far gone.

But this is where strength-based thinking offered us both another path.

I asked her what small actions she could take for herself. We talked about writing letters to elected officials. Maybe submitting an op-ed. Perhaps not sweeping acts of activism, but intentional acts of engagement. As we spoke, something shifted. Her grief remained, but her sense of agency returned. Even quiet action is still action. And small steps, repeated and multiplied, become movements.

This is where change begins. It is not by ignoring injustice, but by refusing to let it silence us.

We model this daily in early childhood by focusing on the strengths and positive contributions of marginalized communities, rather than their challenges. By creating classrooms where equity isn't an add-on, but the foundation. And by practicing advocacy as a daily act, not just an occasional one. That means speaking up in meetings, supporting mission-driven organizations, holding institutions accountable, and using our voices, even the softest ones to demand better.

When we align our actions with our values, whether by mentoring a colleague, choosing where to spend our money, or teaching children that kindness is strength, we create a ripple effect. It may feel small, but small doesn't mean insignificant. Overcoming the divisive "us versus them" mindset is not a one-time fix. It's a practice. A commitment. A way of being.

And it begins where all change begins: in a relationship.

Learning Lessons

My leadership journey took a discouraging turn as my passion for it faded. I was going through the motions, but felt no motivation for the cause. My involvement with the various boards, organizations, and committees I participated in failed to bring me a sense of fulfillment or happiness. I found the meetings to be time-consuming and energy-zapping, resulting in a significant downturn in my overall mood and leaving me feeling frustrated. I struggled with this decision for a long time because of the considerable weight of guilt in the possibility of disappointing others.

Remember my people-pleasing tendencies? I wondered if backing out would damage my leadership abilities or suggest a lack of commitment to the underlying principles of the organization. Would people think of me differently if I resigned?

Even as I took on these leadership roles, my people-pleasing side meant I agonized over every decision, terrified of disappointing someone, which was a major source of my burnout.

Having a substitute teacher available on some days enabled me to attend most daytime meetings while keeping my overall schedule flexible and under control, as well as attend some evening meetings. Many people in my position could not do daytime meetings, and if I did not represent my peers, who would? In theory, I knew I needed to make a change, but I did not know how to withdraw gracefully. This went on for a few years.

My health problems determined what I did. I developed a serious medical condition that manifested as a gradual and troubling loss of my peripheral vision. I experienced headaches more frequently than in the past. The creeping loss of my peripheral vision was alarming.

The diagnosed disease shares a similar clinical presentation with brain tumors, often leading to diagnostic confusion. Let me state for the record that I did not have a brain tumor! I had excess cerebrospinal fluid (CSF) in my brain. CSF flows from the spinal column to the brain, which circulates around its outer layers. Excessive cerebrospinal fluid can exert pressure on the brain and optic nerve, causing various symptoms, including problems with vision, headaches, and other neurological issues. Over many months, I underwent many diagnostic tests to arrive at a conclusive diagnosis.

I began treatment to prevent further vision loss. The neuro-ophthalmologist gave me medication for altitude sickness, a standard prescription for this condition. My doctor explained that the medication could induce considerable drowsiness, detachment, disorientation, and altered taste perception. Starting treatment with a low dosage of medication, I found that after my body adapted to this initial level, the debilitating and crippling pressure headaches would return, thus causing a reassessment of the treatment plan. Characterizing the treatment involved a continuous loop: escalating the medication, observing and assessing the results, and further escalating the dose, as the initial increase did not achieve the desired outcome. Raising my medication to the highest possible dose led to a substantial increase in the severity of the side effects I was already suffering.

My medication's side effects made my workday tough. My difficulty focusing, coupled with late-night meetings across time zones, exacerbated my symptoms.

I found it difficult to keep my appointments, commitments, and schedule accurate. I couldn't commit my energy and focus to these organizations anymore. The organization deserved a person who could meet the needs of the position. These circumstances forced my resignation.

Only years later did I understand the invaluable gift I had presented myself.

Following a series of tests, the final diagnosis revealed intracranial hypertension as the underlying medical issue. After months of medication and tests, my neurologist ordered a CT venogram, a specialized scan using contrast dye to image horizontal brain cross-sections from above. A stenosis disrupted the usual flow and obstructed my brain's normal fluid circulation. This condition was something I was born with, and as the years went by, my condition worsened, but the discovery of a solution brought me immense relief. I was more than ready to stop taking the medication and recover.

While it's true that my body forced the decision, the pause it created gave me something I hadn't realized I needed: space to reflect. For the first time in a long time, I could ask the questions I'd been too busy or too afraid to sit with. Questions like, "What gives me life?" and "Where do I feel most aligned with my work?" The surgery may have treated the physical condition, but it was the stillness that healed something deeper. Looking back, I now see this as a turning point when I began living into Appreciative Inquiry without even knowing the name for it. I wasn't abandoning leadership; I was redefining it on my terms, guided by purpose, presence, and possibility.

I underwent brain surgery that included placement of an intracranial stent, and then I began on the road to recovery.

The moral of the story? If your heart isn't in it, perhaps it's time to move on. I took a step back to assess what brought me joy and where I could best apply my skills. That pause helped me refocus on the organizations I support, not out of obligation, but out of genuine alignment with my values.

My time, energy, and advocacy are now dedicated to two causes: the Life is Good Playmaker Project and the World Forum on Early Care and Education. My interest in these communities predates my knowledge of Appreciative Inquiry.

Looking back, it feels like a kind of foreshadowing, a quiet alignment between who I was becoming and where I was. These organizations embody the spirit of Appreciative Inquiry in both mission and practice. They believe in human potential, in possibility, and in the transformative power of connection. Through them, I have seen how AI can enhance not only programs and systems, but also the lives of those within them. Supporting these causes has brought me personal fulfillment and a deep sense of purpose.

Relationships are at the heart of quality care.

At its core, early childhood education is built on relationships, those between children and caregivers, educators and families, and among the professionals who work to make human systems thrive. I have been fortunate to experience the power of these relationships on a global scale through my involvement with the World Forum Foundation for Early Care and Education (WoFo). The opportunities I have had to teach and collaborate in places like Hawaii, China, and Panama have been nothing short of life-changing. These experiences enriched my teaching practice, broadened my understanding of diverse perspectives, and deepened my appreciation for the universal values we share as educators.

Since 1999, the World Forum Foundation has consistently worked towards its goal of connecting passionate people globally to better children's lives. With an emphasis on fostering dialogue across cultures, languages, and systems, the Forum uplifts a shared vision: to ensure that all children, regardless of where they live, have access to high-quality early care and education. This work has grounded me in purpose and reaffirmed my belief that prioritizing relationships can transform human systems.

The Life is Good Playmaker Project (LIGPP) is a prime example of how we prioritize relationships. Play is how LIGPP promotes joy, optimism, and healing. Playmakers, those trained to build safe, joyful, and empowering environments, reach over one million children annually, many of whom face overwhelming adversity. Their mission is clear: to create a world where all children are surrounded by supportive relationships and positive experiences that foster resilience and well-being. Steve Gross, Chief Playmaker, presented his mission live on stage at TEDx UPenn. Steve's warmth and vibrant energy served as a potent reminder: play isn't mere recreation; it's vital. It offers connection, healing, and empowerment. His storytelling filled the room with light, highlighting the role of optimism and connection in children's thriving, not just surviving.

Both organizations, though different in scope and setting, reflect the essence of Appreciative Inquiry.

I am drawn to people and organizations that look for the positive, believe in people's capacity, and lead with purpose and joy. These aren't just organizations I support, They are communities where my values live and breathe. They continue to remind me that the work we do matters, especially when it's grounded in hope, strengths, and the unwavering belief in what's possible.

Steve reminds us that "The world doesn't need more realists to remind us of how bad and ugly things are. The world needs optimists. Optimists see the good, the bad, and the ugly, but focus on leveraging the good to improve things. When that happens, and people prioritize their ROH (return on humanity) over their return on investment, humanity will evolve faster than most have ever deemed possible." (Gross, 2024)

Ellen Lempereur Greaves, the Senior Director of Program and Learning for the Playmaker Project, stated that decades of research and over thirty years of her playmaker practice have shown her that positive relationships with skilled, loving adults are essential for children's healing. Play is the most effective way to foster these crucial relationships. A strong correlation exists between the number of Adverse Childhood Experiences (ACEs) a child endures and their increased probability of encountering negative consequences in their adult life, highlighting the significant long-term impact of early adversity. The Centers for Disease Control and Prevention (CDC) defines adverse childhood experiences (ACEs) as traumatic events occurring during childhood, and they associate a range of negative consequences with these experiences, including, but not limited to, compromised physical and mental well-being, substance abuse issues, and engagement in high-risk behaviors. Through shared moments of playfulness and fun, we create relationships and connections that buffer against the difficulties and challenges life throws our way.

Playmaker 101's beginning evoked the same intrigue and anticipation I felt starting my Appreciative Inquiry Practitioner course. Through extensive training, early childhood professionals develop skills in using collaborative games, including those with parachutes and beach balls, therapeutically with children, appreciating the unique value of each.

The LIGPP prioritizes its playmakers' self-care. People can use visual play plans to chart their favorite activities and improve their sense of fulfillment. Caregivers of young children are encouraged to relax and have fun by hiking, camping, sewing, crafting, or watching their favorite sport. Adults must engage in renewing, refreshing, and rejuvenating activities to create joyful experiences for children, regardless of the specific activity.

I met with a group of family child care providers during one of our monthly Communities of Practice. For the past several months, we had been focusing on themes of self-awareness and self-care topics that are both timely and needed. Many providers admitted feeling overextended, struggling to reconcile leadership duties with the pressures of running their businesses. A thought stopped me mid-listen: Why the compulsion to do it all?

I asked this out loud, not just to them, but to myself. It stirred something in me. I reflected on my journey, wondering where that inner drive to take on more and more came from. Was I chasing something that would finally make me feel accomplished? Seen? Maybe I thought that if I just did enough, if I led enough, helped enough, stood out enough, it would mean something. Would I finally feel like I was enough? That moment of questioning wasn't about guilt or judgment. It was about getting curious.

What was the motivation I was hoping for? And more importantly, was it rooted in who I truly am, or in who I thought I needed to be?

Choosing the Right Leadership Activities with the Triple R Framework
Leverage the TRF (Relevance, Relationship, Reflection) to assess the suitability of leadership opportunities for an educator based on their strengths, requirements, and current capabilities.

Is this activity meaningful and timely for you or your audience?

Relevance
+ Does this leadership activity align with their current interests, passions, or professional goals?

+ Is it connected to their day-to-day work in a way that makes it feel authentic, not just an add-on?

+ Will it help them build skills they want or need right now?

+ Does it address a genuine need in the program or classroom that they care about?

Relationship

+ Does this activity strengthen trust and support?

+ Does this opportunity honor what you know about this person's strengths and comfort level?

+ Will they feel supported and safe to take risks in this role?

+ Can you provide coaching or co-leadership if needed?

+ Does it encourage healthy connections with teammates or families, instead of isolating them?

Reflection

+ Does this activity nurture growth and self-awareness?

+ Will this experience help the person learn something about themselves or develop confidence?

+ Have you checked in with them about how ready they feel?

+ Are there ways to adjust the task so it's a stretch but not overwhelming?

+ Is there a plan for reflecting afterward to celebrate what went well and what they might do next time?

Quick TRF Leadership Fit Check

Before assigning or taking on a leadership task, ask:

+ Relevant: Is this meaningful for them?

+ Relationship: Will they feel connected and supported?

+ Reflection: Will this grow their skills and identity?

If all three are a "yes" you have a match! If not, adjust the task, offer extra scaffolding, or choose a better fit.

What does "extra scaffolding" mean?

Scaffolding is the support you offer to help someone succeed at a new or challenging task. In leadership, extra scaffolding means providing guidance, modeling, or partnership to set someone up for success.

This could look like:

+ Co-leading the task with them for the first time

+ Giving a simple example or checklist to follow

+ Offering regular check-ins and feedback

+ Breaking the task into smaller, manageable steps

+ Connecting them with a mentor or peer buddy

+ Helping them reflect on what's working along the way

When someone is learning or stretching into a new leadership role, scaffolding helps them feel capable and safe while still giving them space to grow. It builds confidence and keeps the task aligned with the TRF.

Insights in Practice
Shifting from "Us vs. Them" to "All of Us Together"

**AI-Inspired
Questions**

Where in my work or life do I notice an "us vs. them" dynamic? How might I reframe it into "we" or "all of us together"?

When have I felt most connected across differences — and what made that possible?

**Reflective
Exercise**

Bias Journal: This week, notice moments when assumptions, defensiveness, or adversarial thinking arise. Instead of judging yourself, jot them down. Then reframe: What's the common ground here? What strength do I see in the other person or group?

**Practice
Tip**

At your next team meeting or family conference, co-create a shared hope. Try asking: "What is one thing we all want for the children we care for?" Capture the answers visually (sticky notes, poster board, or a digital board). Keep this visible as a reminder that you are working toward the same goal, even when perspectives differ.

Chapter Five

THE STRENGTHS SHIFT

"THE TASK OF LEADERSHIP IS TO CREATE AN
ALIGNMENT OF STRENGTHS... MAKING A SYSTEM'S WEAKNESSES
IRRELEVANT."

-Peter Drucker

Early Childhood Education: What is our future path? Why use a strength-based framework?

Early childhood education is at a critical juncture. The current climate presents significant challenges, including workforce shortages, increased demands on educators, and evolving family dynamics, and a remarkable opportunity: to reimagine the support systems for children, families, and professionals.

Early childhood education is evolving in our vision to be more holistic, inclusive, and empowering by focusing on relationships, equity, and well-being. We need to move away from focusing on problems and instead concentrate on strengths. What works well? What are the possibilities?

Children, educators, and families all carry within them remarkable strengths and untapped potential.

Strengths-based frameworks like Appreciative Inquiry and reflective practice recognize and honor this truth. By focusing on what's working well, we can uplift and empower everyone involved in early childhood education, fostering a strong sense of identity, belonging, and purpose.

Children flourish when their environments celebrate their individuality and encourage self-reliance. The same is true for adults. When we view families as partners, not just recipients of support, we build trust and shared ownership on the learning journey. And when early childhood organizations emphasize possibility over deficiency, they become more resilient, more connected, and far better equipped to reduce burnout and cultivate meaningful change.

In a field often marked by stress and high expectations, focusing on our strengths isn't just a pleasant idea; it's essential. It's how we move from surviving to thriving. Instead of fixing what's broken, we invest in what's best.

Our understanding of early brain development has come a long way over the past few decades, but there's still more to learn. With continued research, we can improve how we work with young children and support their development.

The significant role of emotional intelligence in children's learning and development is often underestimated in our interactions with them. It's not a soft skill.

This transition reflects a deeper understanding of child development and the importance of nurturing the whole child. Yet, it has not come without challenges.

This change has been met with resistance from traditionalists who are committed to outdated measures of success. Prioritizing emotional intelligence, both in ourselves and in the children we care for isn't about abandoning academics. It's about creating the emotional safety and relational capacity that makes real learning possible. "Being emotionally intelligent is key to how one reacts to what life throws. It is a fundamental element of compassion and comprehending the deeper reasons behind other people's actions. It is not the most intelligent people who are the most prosperous or the most fulfilled in life. Many people exel academically yet are socially incompetent and unsuccessful in their careers or intimate relationships." (Frothingham, 2024)

Integrating optimism, Appreciative Inquiry, emotional intelligence, growth mindset, and positive psychology into daily work interactions builds supportive and thriving work environments. These frameworks are not isolated ideas; they're interconnected, reinforcing one another in meaningful ways. When we nurture a mindset rooted in collaboration and shared purpose, we shift from working in silos to working as a cohesive team. In a team-oriented setting, these overlapping elements of curiosity, empathy, resilience, and the belief in potential become essential ingredients for collective success. By infusing these practices into our everyday conversations, decisions, and relationships, we create spaces where people feel valued, energized, and equipped to grow together.

Considering that children's brains are 90% developed by age five, why aren't we introducing these concepts during their formative years? Delaying key emotional intelligence skills instruction until children are older may impede their learning.

Three Experts, Three Points of View

Alyssa Blask Campbell, provides insightful guidance on raising emotionally intelligent children. In her book Tiny Humans, Big Emotions, she writes:

> "When I really pause to consider what I want for my child, for your child, and all the children around us, I want them to have the tools to navigate and process the inevitable hard stuff so they're able to live a life that feels connected, compassionate, and develops them to understand their emotions and develop their skills and know how to navigate their feelings healthily and securely. I want them to be emotionally intelligent."
> (Campbell & Stauble, 2023, p. 13)

Her work reminds us that teaching children how to process big emotions isn't a luxury. It's a foundation for lifelong well-being and meaningful relationships.

Data-driven insights and a focus on long-term impact define the essential perspective of Nobel Prize winner Dr. James J. Heckman. His groundbreaking research at the University of Chicago has shown that high-quality early childhood education, especially programs beginning at birth, produces a 13% return on investment, far surpassing the cited 7–10% ROI for preschool programs focused on ages 3 and 4. The 2016 ABC/CARE study followed children into adulthood and measured improvements across a range of life outcomes: educational attainment, employment, income, physical and mental health, crime reduction, and increased maternal earnings because of accessible child care. As Heckman reaffirmed in 2023, early and comprehensive intervention changes the trajectory of children's lives, and the ripple effect benefits entire communities.

Sarah Truebridge, author of *Resilience Begins with Beliefs*, advocates for a fresh approach to education that recognizes the deep link between cognition and emotion. Recent neuroscience breakthroughs confirm what experienced educators have known: emotions impact attention, motivation, memory, and learning. Truebridge stresses that building on children's strengths unlocks their resilience and academic potential.

Together, these three perspectives underscore a shared truth: investing in early childhood development is not just beneficial, it's essential. Emotional intelligence, economic impact, and integrating social-emotional learning into cognitive development all point to the same conclusion.

Children thrive when we nurture their entire selves; heart, mind, and spirit. And when we do that with intention and care, the benefits ripple outward to families, communities, and society at large. This holistic approach is essential to the spirit of Appreciative Inquiry, which asks us to look for what gives life, what's working well, and how we can build on those strengths to create lasting, meaningful change.

Emotional intelligence, literacy, empathy, and emotional regulation are foundational to resilience. When children (and adults) learn to navigate their internal worlds, they become more capable of forming compassionate relationships and contributing to a culture of care. Emotional regulation is linked to increased empathy, and empathy strengthens our human systems, from classrooms to boardrooms.

When we help children identify and explore the activities that light them up, we're not just teaching skills, we're instilling a lifelong love of learning and a belief in their own capacity to grow and thrive. These are the same principles that empower teams and transform organizations: curiosity, possibility, and a commitment to learning together.

Instilling these crucial skills in young children paves the way for academic excellence and cultivates self-awareness, confidence, and future leadership capabilities. Education becomes more than a system of knowledge; it becomes a practice of inquiry, wonder, and connection. And that, at its core, is the heart of Appreciative Inquiry: seeing what's possible and helping it grow.

Insights in Practice
Strengths, Emotional Intelligence, and the Whole Child

AI-Inspired Questions

When I think about my classroom (or program), what is already working well that supports children's emotional intelligence?

What moments of resilience, curiosity, or compassion have I seen in children or colleagues this week?

Reflective Exercise

Joy + Strengths Journal: For one week, jot down one joyful moment you observed in a child and one strength you noticed in a colleague each day. At the end of the week, reflect: What patterns do I see? How does focusing on strengths change my own energy and outlook?

Practice Tip

During a staff or family meeting, begin with a strengths circle. Invite each person to share one strength they've noticed in a child, colleague, or family member. Capture these on chart paper or a whiteboard to keep visible — a collective reminder that thriving grows when we notice and name strengths.

Chapter Six

THE ARCHITECTURE OF POSSIBILITY

"WE LIVE IN THE WORLD OUR QUESTIONS CREATE."

-David Cooperrider

Frameworks like SOAR (Strengths, Opportunities, Aspirations, and Results), the 5D Cycle, and the 5I Cycle offer structured pathways for planning and change. The Triple R Framework, however, provides something different, a mindset lens. Centered on Relevance, Relationships, and Reflection, it grounds these tools in a human-centered, strengths-based practice that speaks directly to the heart of early childhood education. It reminds us that lasting change is not only about strategy, but about connection, meaning, and the courage to pause and reflect.

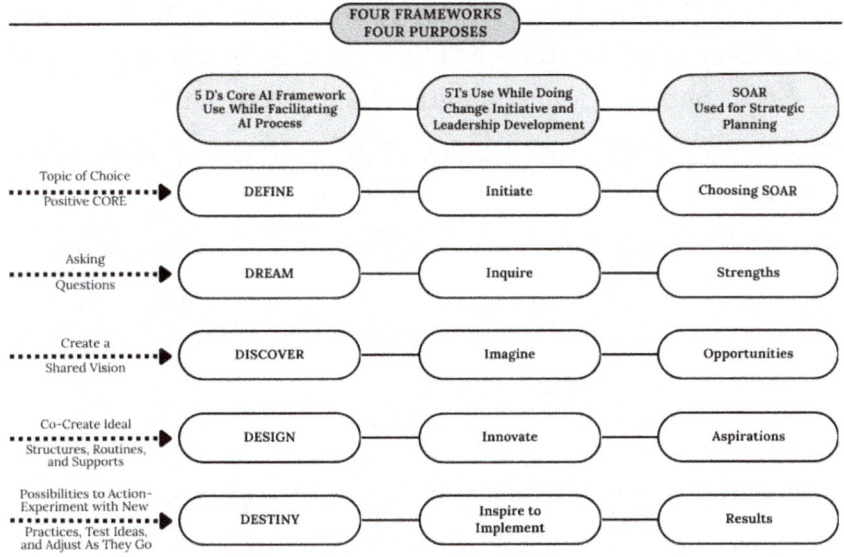

FOUR FRAMEWORKS
FOUR PURPOSES

	5 D's Core AI Framework Use While Facilitating AI Process	5I's Use While Doing Change Initiative and Leadership Development	SOAR Used for Strategic Planning
Topic of Choice Positive CORE	DEFINE	Initiate	Choosing SOAR
Asking Questions	DREAM	Inquire	Strengths
Create a Shared Vision	DISCOVER	Imagine	Opportunities
Co-Create Ideal Structures, Routines, and Supports	DESIGN	Innovate	Aspirations
Possibilities to Action- Experiment with New Practices, Test Ideas, and Adjust As They Go	DESTINY	Inspire to Implement	Results

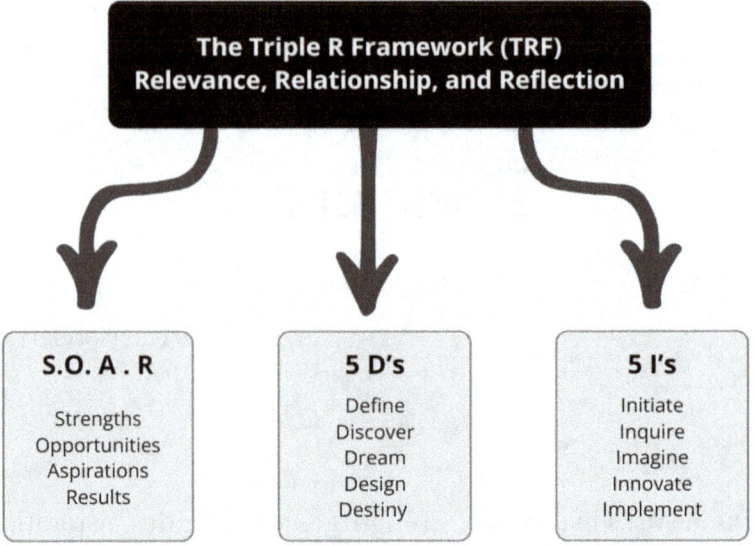

Standard (SWOT) Strengths, Weaknesses, Opportunities, and Threats analyses are a common business practice. SWOT analysis employs a hierarchical planning method, neglecting diverse perspectives.

The strategic planning tool known as SWOT analysis facilitates the evaluation of an organization's internal strengths and weaknesses, as well as its external opportunities and threats. The company's strengths are its established brand, expert personnel, and innovative product offerings. Limitations, whether stemming from a lack of resources or outdated technology, are inherent weaknesses. Organizational opportunities concentrate on helpful factors, such as emerging markets, prevailing trends, and collaborative partnerships.

Threats are risks outside your control that could block progress, cause losses, or create obstacles. These could be situations like budget cuts, new laws or regulations increasing burdens, or a change in preferences that families are seeking.

Focusing on these four key areas in a SWOT analysis allows businesses to develop strategies that capitalize on strengths, address weaknesses, exploit opportunities, and avoid threats.

When management is top-down, employee morale and innovation suffer because their input and flexibility are disregarded. In large corporations and non-profits, many employees lack influence over decisions impacting their positions.

Early childhood isn't the only time when people feel powerless. In many large systems, change is frequently forced on people rather than implemented. When decisions are made without input from those closest to the work, the result is often confusion, resistance, and disengagement. To shift this dynamic, we need planning tools that not only include people's voices, but also center on their strengths and aspirations. That's where the SOAR framework comes in.

By focusing on strengths, opportunities, aspirations, and results, the SOAR model leverages Appreciative Inquiry. SOAR was created by Jackie Stavros and her colleagues, and aligns strategic planning and positive psychology. This framework is a strengths-based alternative to SWOT (Strengths, Weaknesses, Opportunities and Threats). SOAR is often used to design or reaffirm a program's mission and vision. This framework can guide strategic planning that involves teachers, families, and administrators. It is a way to help in identifying team strengths and community assets before expanding services. SOAR centers what's working, building confidence and cohesion. This framework values community voice, especially from families and front-line educators. It inspires future visioning, even in the face of limited resources, and it drives actionable results without deficit thinking.

Let's look at a common challenge in programs.

Example: Using SOAR to Strengthen Family Engagement in an Early Childhood Center

Context:

A preschool director wants to improve family engagement, not because families are disengaged, but because there's potential to go deeper and build stronger partnerships and create more meaningful, two-way communication between home and school.

S-Strengths

The team begins by identifying what's already working:

+ "What do we do well when it comes to family connections?"

+ "What makes families feel welcomed here?"

+ Families regularly attend family events like potlucks and parent-teacher conferences.

+ Teachers build warm, trusting relationships with families during daily drop-off and pick-up.

+ A few families are actively involved in classroom volunteering and community events.

O–Opportunities

Next, they explore opportunities to expand and deepen engagement.

+ "What possibilities exist if we strengthen two-way communication?"

+ "How might we make all families feel more like partners?"

> Using families' home languages more intentionally in communication and curriculum.

> Inviting families to share their skills or cultural traditions with the class.

> Creating a more flexible format for family input (surveys, suggestion boxes, informal chats).

A–Aspirations

The team imagines what's possible:

+ "What relationship do we aspire to have with families?"

+ "What would it look like if every family felt fully included and valued?"

> A community where families feel seen as co-educators and leaders in their child's learning.

> A shared culture of belonging, where family voices shape programming.

> Stronger home-school connections that support children's identity and well-being.

R–Results

They identify measurable goals.

+ "How will we know we're moving toward our vision?"

+ "What data or stories can help us celebrate progress?"

> Host monthly family spotlight sessions where parents share something about their culture or family life.

> Increase family response rates on annual surveys by 40%.

> Track family involvement across different formats (virtual, in-person, written) to ensure accessibility.

This SOAR process not only centers on strengths and possibility, it creates momentum for inclusive, sustainable, and meaningful improvement that uplifts everyone in the community.

For positive, strengths-based change, the 5 Ds of Appreciative Inquiry: Define, Discover, Dream, Design, and Destiny/Deliver are the most effective approach. This framework is especially helpful when you're looking to engage people in meaningful dialogue, co-create solutions, and build momentum from what's already working.

This framework is a powerful tool when the goal is trust-building, strengthening a team, and reconnecting passion and purpose. Especially when there's tension between teams (admin vs. teachers, child care providers vs. policymakers, families vs. educators) this framework is helpful in creating a shared language, mutual understanding, and a common goal. Questions receive meticulous curation within this framework. Here is an example of the 5-D cycle in use.

The next several pages will outline ways to use these cycles. None of this intended to be done in one day or one week and could take awhile to work through the process.

Reimagining Outdoor Play Spaces Through the 5D Cycle

Background information:
Rather than start with what's missing, the team uses Appreciative Inquiry to envision what's possible.

1. Define
Topic of Inquiry:

"How can we create outdoor play spaces that inspire wonder, support whole-child development, and reflect our program's values?"

The team agrees to focus on outdoor spaces as places for learning, belonging, and joy, not just physical activity.

2. Discover

What's already working? Where are the strengths?

+ Children love using sticks, rocks, and loose parts to build.

+ Educators notice more cooperation and problem-solving outside.

+ Families often comment that their children talk about outdoor time the most.

+ Teachers recall a day when mud play led to rich storytelling and collaboration.

"When have our outdoor spaces felt magical, joyful, or deeply engaging?"

"What do we already do well outside that supports children's growth?"

3. Dream

What do we hope for? What could outdoor time look and feel like?

The team imagines:

+ A "nature nook" with stumps, logs, and native plants.

+ A sound exploration area with wind chimes and recycled instruments.

+ A flexible outdoor art space that changes with the seasons.

+ A co-created "child-led play zone" built with kids' input.

"If anything were possible, what kind of outdoor play space would we create together?"

"What would the children be doing, feeling, and saying out there?"

4. Design

What needs to be in place to make the dream a reality?

Together, the team:

+ Maps out under-used corners of the yard to repurpose.

+ Partners with families to gather natural materials and tools.

+ Sets a rotating schedule so that each classroom has time to co-create outdoor play structures.

+ Build in reflection time during staff meetings to notice changes and share stories.

"What changes will move us closer to our dream?"

"What actions can we take together, starting small and growing over time?"

5. Destiny / Deliver

How do we bring it to life and sustain the energy?

+ Monthly "outdoor inspiration walks" become part of the routine for educators.

+ Children's photos and quotes about outdoor play are displayed and shared with families.

+ A "Wonder Wall" is created for kids and staff to document discoveries.

+ The team commits to seasonal reflections to evaluate and celebrate how outdoor time evolves.

+ "How will we keep the momentum going?"

+ "How can we continue learning from the children and nature itself?"

This example highlights how Appreciative Inquiry can turn a typical environment improvement process into a joyful, collaborative redesign, rooted in strengths, values, and shared vision.

The Five I's in Practice

Context:

A preschool director notices that daily transitions (especially from outdoor play back into the classroom) often lead to frustration, tears, and chaos. Instead of defaulting to "fixing the problem," she decides to guide her team through the

Five I's Framework.

1. Initiate – Create the container and invite curiosity.

The director calls a staff meeting, saying:

"I have noticed transitions can be tough for kids and staff. Let's work together to explore what's happening and what might help."

This sets the tone: open, collaborative, and strengths-based.

2. Inquire – Ask appreciative, generative questions.

Teachers share stories of when transitions did go well. One recalls a day when children sang a silly cleanup song together, and another mentions when an assistant gave kids "special jobs" (line leader, door holder) and transitions went more smoothly.

The director asks: "What made those moments work? What strengths were we leaning on?"

3. Imagine – Co-create a vision of what's possible.
The team imagines transitions where children feel calm, supported, and even joyful. They describe a vision: children moving inside with purpose, teachers staying regulated, and everyone feeling ready for the next activity.

4. Innovate – Design and test small, creative experiments.
Together, they decide to try:

+ A transition song chosen by the children.

+ Helper roles rotated daily to give kids ownership.

+ A "calm-down job" (like carrying the transition mascot, a stuffed animal to the circle).

They agree to test these ideas for two weeks and observe what happens.

5. Inspire – Share successes and ripple learning outward.
After two weeks, teachers celebrate how transitions have shifted: fewer tears, more laughter, and smoother routines. One teacher

even shares a story of a child who started leading the transition song on their own.

The director highlights these successes in a staff newsletter and encourages teachers to share with families: "Ask your child to sing their transition song at home!"

Outcome:
By moving through the Five I's, the team did not just "fix a problem." They created ownership, tested fresh ideas, and built a culture of possibility. Transitions became an opportunity for connection instead of conflict.

Using Appreciative Inquiry 5 D's to create a Vision, Philosophy, and Mission

I have worked with many programs that have been in business for years. When we dive deep into the challenges that the program continues to be up against, we realize that the vision, mission and philosophy do not reflect the current values of the program. These should be revisited every few years to check if this is still the mission you want to put out into the world.

Early childhood programs rely on their vision, mission, and philosophy to define their purpose, guide their actions, and shape their daily activities. Developing this framework requires several meetings, and it should not be rushed.

For children, families, and the community, the vision statement sets forth the program's aspirational, long-term goals. The tone encourages a collaborative spirit and shared goals, setting a forward-thinking path for stakeholders. The vision statement's priority: It establishes the program's aspirational goal, defining its purpose and desired impact. Aligning all statements with the program's long-term direction and ideals starts with the vision.

The program's philosophy statement details its guiding beliefs and principles in early childhood education. It reflects the program's values, understanding of child development, and commitment to fostering meaningful relationships with children and families. These statements align all stakeholders and create a shared identity and purpose that can adapt to the community's needs.

Focusing on daily activities, the program details its core purpose and how it achieves its vision.

While SOAR and the AI cycles are structured processes for strategic planning and change, the TRF helps educators and leaders stay grounded in what matters most: relevance to their daily context, strong relationships among stakeholders, and reflection as a driver for meaningful progress. In early childhood education, these methodologies work best when used together, combining structure with humanity, and planning with purpose. (Wholeness Principle)

What the process looks like:

Define the Purpose and Scope

Goal: Develop statements that reflect the program's values, mission, and philosophy.

To ensure inclusivity, key stakeholders like educators, families, administrators, and older children (where appropriate) should be involved.

Discover: Explore Strengths

Interview, focus groups, or surveys to identify:

Key strengths of the program are its community partnerships, nurturing environment, and innovative practices.

Moments when the program was at its best.

The shared values and beliefs of stakeholders.

Dream: Envision the Ideal Future

Facilitate visioning sessions where participants imagine the best possible future for the program.

Identify themes in participants' visions to inform the mission and philosophy.

Design: Craft the Statements

Consider the program's fundamental principles and beliefs. Keep your language short and to the point.

Define the program's purpose and whom it serves.

Articulate the approach to education, guiding theories, and practices.

Deliver: Test and Refine

Share drafts of the statements with stakeholders for feedback.

Revise as needed to ensure alignment with the program's identity and goals.

Destiny: Embed and Sustain

Integration: Incorporate the value, mission, and philosophy into daily practices, hiring processes, curriculum planning, and family communication.

Celebrations: use them as benchmarks to celebrate successes and guide decision-making.

Reflection: Review, reflect, and refine so that it grows with the program.

Example of statements using appreciative language:

Value Statement:

"We value the unique strengths of every child and family, embracing diversity as a catalyst for growth."

Mission Statement:

"Our goal is to create joyful learning environments where children thrive, families feel supported, and educators are empowered to innovate."

Our philosophy centers on play-based, inquiry-driven learning. We see children as capable learners; we are here to nurture their curiosity, creativity, and resilience.

Principles, Visions, Missions, and Assumptions

The Oxford Dictionary defines "principles" as a fundamental truth or proposition that is a foundation for a system of beliefs or a chain of reasoning. Other related words are truth, proposition, concept, idea, theory, postulate, and assumption. What about a person's principles?

Moral principles are guidelines that people live by to make sure they are doing the right thing. These include things like honesty, fairness, and equality. A person's morality or moral principles can differ from someone else's because they depend on their upbringing and what is important to them. (Cunic, 2024)

Over the past 30 years, I mentored many teachers, monitoring their progress as they worked toward earning their Child Development Associate Credential. My observations encompassed various teaching methods implemented with students spanning a significant age range. I observed substantial differences in how teachers taught and cared for children because of the wide range of teaching styles and classroom environments designed for young children. When lead teachers have classroom autonomy, they align their visions, missions, and principles more closely with overall program goals. The educators I worked with frequently discussed the program's systemic obstacles they encountered while designing lessons and managing their classrooms. I talked to them about their beliefs to see if they matched the program's goals. More often than not, the teacher did not know the program's philosophy, mission, and vision.

Understanding this key information is essential when determining whether a program, school, or organization aligns with your values. In conversations with educators, a common theme emerged: the organization's core mission was often not a prioritized conversation with many potential employees, and sometimes the directors could not articulate the program's values.

A vision statement acts as a guiding star for your company, motivating your team and directing your organization's growth. It's not something to be dismissed. A vision statement should be co-written by multiple company stakeholders and will require a significant time investment. (Asana, 2024)

See the templates in Appendix E for writing these statements.

Insights in Practice
Putting the Frameworks Into Action

AI-Inspired Questions

Which framework (TRF, SOAR, 5-D, or 5-I) feels most relevant to my current work or challenge? Why?

How might I use one of these frameworks not just in professional settings, but in my daily life?

Framework Match: Think of one challenge or opportunity you're facing (for example: staff morale, family engagement, or planning PD). Write it at the top of a page. Then, test-drive each framework briefly:

TRF (Relevance, Relationship, Reflection): Which "R" feels most important here?

Reflective Exercise

SOAR (Strengths, Opportunities, Aspirations, Results): What strengths can we leverage?

5-D Cycle: Where are we in the cycle — Discover, Dream, Design, Destiny, or Define?

5-I's: How might Initiate, Inquire, Imagine, Innovate, and Inspire apply?

Notice which framework opens up the most energy or clarity for you.

Introduce one framework at your next team meeting in a simple way:

+ Start with a SOAR brainstorm.

+ Frame your agenda with the Triple R Framework™ (Is this relevant? How are we building relationships? Where will we reflect?).

+ Use the 5-D cycle for strategic planning, even on a small scale like rethinking transitions.

+ Try the 5-I's to structure a family engagement initiative.

+ Start small, but commit to experimenting. The more you use these frameworks, the more natural they become.

Practice Tip

Chapter Seven

COMPLIANCE TO CONNECTION

"CONNECTION IS WHY WE'RE HERE; IT IS WHAT GIVES PURPOSE
AND MEANING TO OUR LIVES."

-Brené Brown

Suppose our program structures embodied the principles we claim to uphold? What if connection, collaboration, and curiosity were more than ideals; they were the foundation of how we lead, learn, and grow together?

So often in early childhood settings, staff meetings feel like something to endure. They are packed with compliance updates, licensing reminders, and to-do lists. But what if we reimagined those meetings as something more; spaces for building culture, recognizing strengths, and inviting ownership?

Imagine this:

+ A different teaching team plans and leads each meeting.

+ A clipboard circulates during the week, inviting staff to shape the agenda.

+ The topics? Real celebrations, persistent challenges, thoughtful questions.

+ The format? Rooted in collaboration, not top-down directives.

+ The impact? A staff culture that feels alive, participatory, and purposeful.

Culture doesn't happen by accident. It's designed; by every interaction, system, and unspoken norm. This chapter is about choosing connection over compliance and making design decisions that nourish the culture where people want to stay and grow.

The strengths-focused method involves recognizing and appreciating personal and group qualities. This focus encourages appreciation and motivation within the team, establishing a collaborative atmosphere. Starting with a "what went well" segment allows staff to reflect on successes, recognize contributions, and build confidence in their capabilities. By reframing issues, team members find chances to innovate and find solutions. This not only promotes a more optimistic atmosphere but also enhances problem-solving by tapping into the skills and perspectives of the group. Using inclusive, strength-based processes builds trust and encourages all team members to participate.

Test this out at your next staff meeting:

+ Ask the team to imagine success in a specific project.

+ This process builds momentum and accountability, paired with clear action steps and recognition of each person's strengths.

+ This will help create a culture of positivity and collaboration, making staff meetings more effective, enjoyable, and meaningful for everyone involved.

See the template at the end of the book. Appendix D.

Administrators and supervisors should handle individual issues apart from staff meetings.

For instance, if someone overhears a teacher snapping at a family, an ineffective response in the moment would be to say, "You can't speak to people in that manner."

After the family leaves and there is a free moment a person can say, "Hey, are you doing all right? You seem a bit off." I overheard your conversation with a family this morning, and it seemed tense." This opens the door to understanding what might be happening with the teacher. Perhaps their response would detail a frantic morning, a child's tantrum, a rushed breakfast, and the sting of spilled coffee adding to the stress of a chaotic morning commute. That sounds like a rough start to the day, filled with anxiety and unforeseen problems. I want to help this teacher overcome challenges and move forward with renewed purpose and optimism.

What I have learned in life is that repair is vital when things like this happen. I'll follow up once their breathing has slowed and they've settled into a quiet rhythm.

I would approach with intentional curiosity, "Since we last talked, have you had a chance to speak with that family?" Waiting enables better planning and resource allocation, leading to more effective handling of the situation.

In their book Conversations Worth Having, Jackie Stavros and Cheri Torres highlight the importance of determining whether our conversations are appreciative or depreciative.

Trust and value are built through appreciative conversations that foster understanding and collaboration, while depreciative conversations can feel critical and lead to conflict. A supportive, empathetic approach with the teacher, avoiding blame, fosters appreciation and benefits all.

Curiosity plays an important role in these interactions. A curious conversational approach indicates our desire to grasp the other person's perspective, feelings, and lived experiences. This curiosity shifts the focus from blame or criticism to exploration and problem-solving. For instance, instead of accusing someone of being dismissive or short-tempered, try asking, "Can you share more about how you're feeling?" This defuses tension and shows empathy, encouraging the other person to feel seen and heard.

Direct communication helps to build psychological safety. People are more likely to take risks, share their concerns, or admit mistakes when they know the purpose behind the communication is supportive rather than punitive.

This also sets an example of the conduct we want to see in others, thus promoting a culture of respect and collaboration. *Empathy creates connection.*

Stavros and Torres (Conversations Worth Having) note the exhausting nature of depreciative conversations, leading to alienation and depletion. Research in positive psychology has found that focusing on what is wrong or zeroing in on problems in order to fix them narrows our cognitive bandwidth. It restricts access to the very skills we need for creativity, critical thinking, and effective problem-solving. Unconstructive conversations stifle innovation, decrease productivity, and lead to disengagement (Stavros & Torres, 2018, p. 30).

I learned this firsthand through my experience with a longtime employee.

Let's call her Judy. Judy's words were candid to a fault. Her honesty, while rooted in good intentions, often came across as curt or insensitive.

Early on, I could have responded with criticism or asked her to soften her tone without deeper inquiry. Instead, I got curious. I saw her communication not as a problem to fix, but as an opportunity to understand. I asked questions, I listened, and I discovered that beneath her sharp edges were significant personal challenges. That experience taught me something foundational: grace and curiosity must live at the center of our values if we want to create a culture of empathy and growth.

My definition of program values evolved, encompassing both children's emotional support (even during minor crises like sock meltdowns) and adult support throughout various difficulties. Conversations worth having are not always easy, but they are grounded in curiosity and connection. They teach us how to stay engaged, even when it would be easier to correct or withdraw.

Leadership especially relies on this principle. Imagine a team meeting where a teacher seems disengaged, with arms crossed, not contributing, avoiding eye contact. A reactive leader might interpret this as laziness or resistance and call it out in front of the group. But that approach risks shame, resentment, and further disconnection.

A perceptive leader may take the teacher aside afterward and comment, "I sensed you were detached during the meeting earlier. Is everything alright? I just want to check in." That simple question opens the door to understanding. Maybe the teacher just received tough news, is feeling unheard in recent meetings, or is overwhelmed by a classroom challenge.

Leaders foster regulation, reflection, and repair by being curious instead of judgmental. They send the message: You matter more than your moment. As Stavros and Torres remind us, appreciative conversations build trust and foster collaboration. They shift our focus from blame to possibility and transform moments of tension into opportunities for connection and growth.

In all relationships, honest communication is key to trust and strength. Clear communication removes the guesswork and assumptions, preventing conflict and miscommunication.

A curious approach to conversation shows interest in another's feelings, experiences, and perspective. Focusing on this interest inspires exploration and problem-solving, not blame or criticism. For example, try asking, "Tell me more about your feelings."

Shifting from Correction to Curiosity
This move from correction to curiosity, from blame to

understanding goes beyond mere communication strategy. It's a mindset. One that Jackie Kelm, in her work on Appreciative Living, describes as focusing on what gives life, even in difficult circumstances. Kelm expands the principles of Appreciative Inquiry beyond organizational development and into everyday life, showing us that when we notice strengths, affirm what's working, and respond with appreciation, we don't just change conversations; we change lives.

Appreciative Living is about training our attention toward possibility. It doesn't mean ignoring problems or bypassing challenges. Rather, it invites us to approach those challenges by first recognizing what is good, what's strong, and what's already working. Unknowingly, I practiced Appreciative Living when I engaged with Judy's ideas instead of rejecting them. I support Kelm's belief that minor, purposeful adjustments can yield substantial improvements in relationships, workplaces, and communities.

This mindset is equally vital when supporting educators who are overwhelmed. Asking "What's going on?" instead of "What's wrong with you?" signals a belief that people are doing the best they can with what they have. It's a way of holding space for others while trusting that strength and resilience are still present, even when they're hard to see. As Kelm writes, living with appreciation helps us "create more of what we want" not by force, but by attention, gratitude, and the belief in potential.

By integrating the work of both Stavros and Torres and Jackie Kelm, we see that the conversations we choose, and the perspectives we adopt, have lasting influence, not just on performance, but on how people feel about themselves and each other. Whether in a classroom, a staff meeting, or a one-on-one conversation, appreciation isn't fluff. It's a fuel. And when we learn to live and lead from that place, we create a culture where growth is not only possible, but inevitable.

Kelm wrote the book The Joy of Appreciative Living and created the Appreciative Living Three-Step Process. (Kelm, 2014)

+ Appreciate what is

+ Imagine the ideal

+ Act toward the ideal

It is a cycle. In the center is the positive core.

Let's look at this process in action.

I met with her twice; the first was to dig into some of my obstacles. At least, I saw them as weaknesses. We had monthly coaching calls that were part of the AI course we did over the year, and Jackie was one of the first experts we met. The day was Friday, and we were on a conference call with our class. I remember her talking a bit about her work and how Appreciative Inquiry aided her through some significant health issues, and how she helped thousands of people grow as she did. I did not grasp at the time the transformative effect her work with me would have on my outlook.

Jackie asked if there was something she could help us with. I waited, and when no one spoke up, I finally said I had a challenge to share. Jackie invited me to describe what I was experiencing. I explained that I was teaching children ages six weeks to five years old in my early childhood program and that, for reasons I couldn't quite explain, I dreaded Mondays. It sounded a little silly, but it was real.

"By Friday," I explained, "Monday has already filled me with dread." I couldn't seem to shake it. She asked me how I felt about that specific situation on a scale of one to five or zero to five. I might have gone negative if there had been a negative number, but I said 0. She asked me what I was feeling and what emotions I was feeling, and I talked to her about the dread of how I loathed Mondays. I would plan nothing for Monday because I always knew it would be a tough day. The children would show up overtired, over-sugared, and with a drained battery from their weekend. I assumed they had no consistent schedule. The day dissolved into meltdowns, tantrums, and a bitterly contested naptime.

Jackie then asked me how I wanted to feel. I told her I wanted to feel grounded and balanced. My goal was to feel confident in handling challenging behaviors and prevent a single issue from ruining my entire day. She asked me, "If you were to name four words, what would they be?" I said, "Balanced, grounded, refreshed, and joyful."

She said my next step was on those Fridays when I started thinking about Mondays. She urged me to say those words to cement them as a mantra. I repeated "balanced, grounded, refreshed, reflective, and joyful" for that entire weekend" every time I thought about Monday. I will admit I was skeptical. How would this make Mondays different? I persisted.

That meeting was on a Friday. I already had the Monday dreads. I followed her directions and repeated the mantra over the weekend, and when I went to bed on Sunday night, I fell asleep while still repeating the mantra.

Monday came, and I thought little about repeating those words; the day came and went and went well. My skepticism settled upon me once again. It couldn't have happened so simply.

Dread came over to me the following Friday. Once more, I heeded Jackie's advice and began with the same mantra. I did what Jackie said again and started with the same mantra. I would move on to the next task, whatever it was, over the weekend, and every time Monday, dread came into my head. I would repeat.

Again, Monday came, and it was fine.

A few weeks later, I had to write a reflection as part of our learning during our AI course. Because I was unsure of a topic. My time with Jackie became the subject of my writing. I discussed the process, what I did each weekend, and the results. I discussed my planned words, actions, and feelings. At that very moment, I was sitting there typing in my journal, and I had an epiphany.

At that moment, I had the realization that what I thought before was that children were showing up overtired, oversugared, and dysregulated. I had decided that this was how they were going to show up. The first time someone had a meltdown, in my head, "Here we go, a shitty Monday." We talk about a glass being half full or half empty. My glass was not half full or half empty. On Mondays, it was empty. I decided on that. I had stomped on the metaphorical cup and couldn't pour anything into it.

This was about me, not the children. I manifested a dreadful Monday by deciding it would be so on Friday night. No behavioral distinctions emerged between Monday and other weekdays. That was my daily approach to those challenges. I realized that this practice regulated and prepared me for the day. I was ready to deal with every challenge that came before me. While this seems so simple, it has plagued me for years. While it looks simple to change a fixed mindset, it can be challenging.

This story illustrates how Jackie Kelm's Appreciative Living Three-Step Process. Appreciate What Is, Imagine the Ideal, and Act Toward the Ideal. This embodies the principles of Appreciative Inquiry.

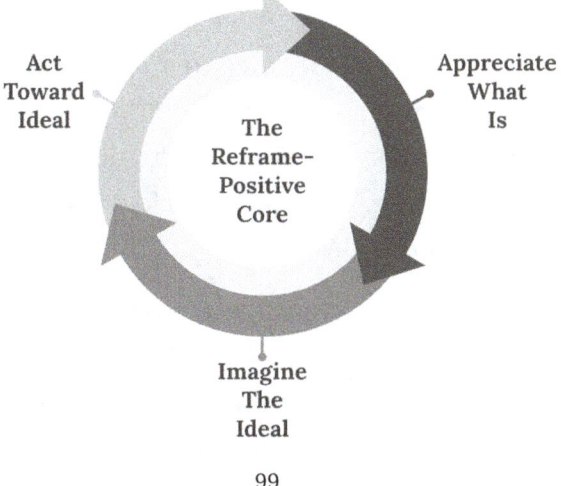

"Appreciate What Is" Jackie helps me reflect on my dread of Mondays by guiding me to articulate and rate my emotions without judgment of the underlying mindset contributing to my struggle. Instead of viewing the challenge as external (children being dysregulated), I recognize it as an internal issue, creating growth space. This first step helps me identify the positive core, shifting the conversation from problems to possibilities.

"Imagine the Ideal" engages positive visualization. Jackie invited me to name my desired emotional state—"balanced, grounded, refreshed, and joyful." Envisioning how I want to feel starts an immediate shift in perspective, sparking optimism and motivation. By focusing on what could be rather than what is, I built a vision of a better Monday.

The process creates a hopeful narrative that can inspire change.

"Act Toward the Ideal" I implement intentional actions aligned with my vision. Jackie's advice to repeat the positive mantra over the weekend becomes a practical strategy for replacing negative thought patterns with empowering ones. Over time, I realized that the key to changing my experience lies in my mindset, not in external circumstances.

This focus connects internal attitudes with external behaviors and highlights the power of positive emotions to broaden perspectives and build resilience. By appreciating what is, envisioning what could be, and acting with intention, I learned to move from a place of dread to one of balance and joy. Appreciative Inquiry principles show us that ingrained challenges can be transformed into opportunities for growth and renewal, not only at a personal level, but within entire organizations and communities.

To turn this personal mindset into meaningful, lasting progress in early childhood settings, we must also understand how change works at a systemic level. Understanding the historical roots of our early childhood systems is essential for building or leading strengths-based programs that honor the past, address inequities, and create environments that are respectful, inclusive, and sustainable for everyone they touch.

Grief in Disguise: Understanding Resistance to Change

I developed and delivered a series of trainings throughout Vermont. The focus was on providing early childhood educators with how-to guidance on advocating for children who needed services or advocating for change to the early education system. It involved meeting them where they were on their journey and recognizing what they were already doing for children and families and encouraging them to stretch their skills. This particular group of educators was resistant to change. It felt like trying to move a brick wall.

At first, I did not grasp their resistance. The recent changes in the state's child care regulations had left many educators feeling stuck, angry, and unheard. Their frustration did not come out of nowhere. It was rooted in a deep sense of betrayal stemming from an early version of the proposed child care regulations. That initial draft had been created with little to no educator input. The process felt top-down and impersonal, leaving many early childhood professionals feeling invisible and devalued.

This sense of exclusion created a narrative that took hold: no one asked us. No one cares what we think. And like many narratives formed in the absence of information, it hardened into resentment, even after the context changed.

What the educators did not yet know was that the first (early) draft of the new regulations had been scrapped. When Reva Murphy stepped into her role as Deputy Commissioner of the Child Development Division, she inherited an almost broken process, complete, but deeply flawed. She made the bold decision to halt the process and start over. Her aim was clear: build trust, not just compliance.

Reva formed stakeholder committees that included educators, program leaders, and family care providers. They reviewed each section of the regulations with care and intention. Once a new draft emerged, the state held listening sessions to gather feedback from across the field. This approach differed: transparent, inclusive, and prioritizing worker input in policy.

By the time I met with this group of educators, the hurt from the earlier draft was still fresh. They hadn't yet connected the dots between what had been done to them and what was now being done with them. Their anger made sense because the wound had not yet been named or healed.

The following week, to help us move forward, I did some research on change theory and returned to the training with the Kübler-Ross model of grief in hand. I presented its adaptation for navigating professional change, outlining each phase and how our behaviors might show up in response.

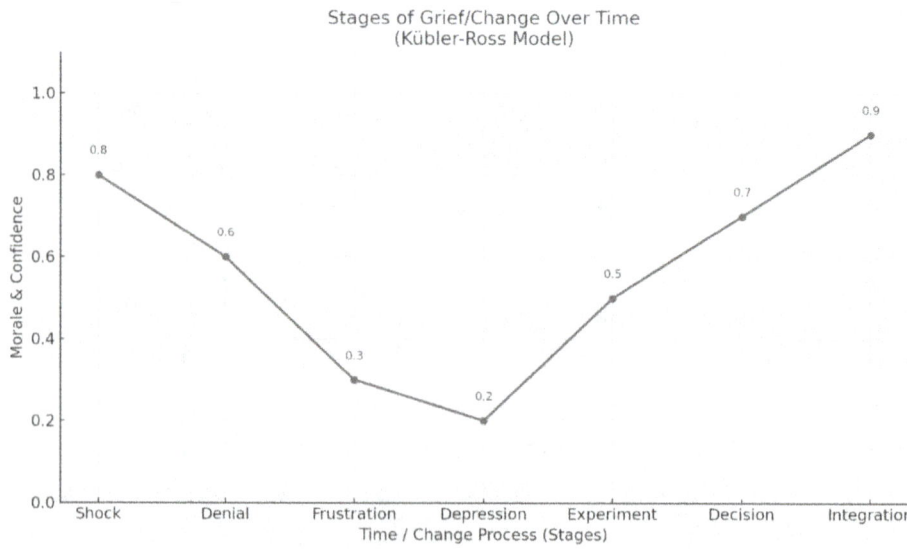

Stages of Grief/Change Over Time
(Kübler-Ross Model)

The Grief Model Applied to Change

Denial: "This isn't really happening."

Anger: "I'm furious and overwhelmed."

Bargaining: "Maybe we can just keep some things the same."

Depression: "This is harder than I thought."

Acceptance: "Okay, this is happening. What now?"

I acknowledged the reality many were facing: that these regulatory changes had come all at once, and for many, it felt like too much to do. Some were encountering the changes for the first time; others had struggled to adapt. Together, we used the grief model not to diagnose, but to reflect. And while some participants were skeptical of applying a grief framework to professional change, they saw their experiences mirrored in the model and many found it validating.

We explored how people often feel disoriented, even angry, during large-scale changes, especially when they've had little say. Resistance was grief in disguise.

As I shared more about the regulation history, Reva's decision to restart the process with community voices at the center, many of the educators were surprised. The narrative shifted. This wasn't about ignoring them. It was about reconnecting to the part of the process that had, in fact, been designed for them.

That shift, acknowledging the past while making space for new understanding opened the door to healing and growth.

Beyond the Checklist: Teaching That Connects and Inspires (TRF)

The TRF is woven throughout this story. When teachers felt disconnected from the proposed changes, it signaled a need to pause and restore. Relevance; to help educators see how the revisions connected to their daily realities and to what mattered most for children and families. Through ongoing dialogue and shared decision-making, relationships were strengthened across sectors, fostering trust and co-regulation in a time of change. And by inviting reflection through committees and public forums, the process honored the collective wisdom of the field, ensuring that final decisions were rooted in both reflection and community identity. In doing so, Reva and her team transformed a top-down regulatory rewrite into a meaningful, strengths-based process grounded in the very principles that sustain effective early childhood systems.

In the Relationship part of the TRF: Using the Kübler-Ross model, I had validated and welcomed their emotions. With that emotional acknowledgment, the regulations felt more accessible than overwhelming. When people feel heard, they can move through the process of acceptance. After sharing their concerns, many realized that they were already doing much of what the new rules asked of them. They just needed to formalize those practices into policy.

Understanding large-scale change is essential. When people understand why change is happening and feel included in how it happens, they are more likely to accept and engage with it. That was true for this group. I invited Reva to meet with them. She arrived well-prepared, and the conversation was thoughtful, structured, and respectful. The women expressed their concerns, and Reva validated their feelings during a difficult transition.

Their shift wasn't just about accepting a new set of regulations, it was about reclaiming their voice in a system that had once excluded them. When people feel seen, heard, and valued, resistance begins to dissolve. This group did not just adapt; they evolved. And that evolution came from being invited into the process, not pushed through it. Understanding that change can be collaborative, not something done to you, but something created with you, was a turning point. And yet, even with new insight, one truth remained: change is hard. Especially when it asks us to unlearn what's familiar.

My friend, Alyssa often shares a car seat analogy that sticks with me and I use quite often in explaining ideas to people that have evolved. She says, "Just because my parents used a car seat for me in the early '90s doesn't mean it is the best car seat in 2025. We know more now."

And she's right. Just as we wouldn't settle for outdated safety measures in a moving vehicle, we can't afford to rely on outdated practices when supporting our youngest learners. This analogy is more than a comparison. It's a reminder that change, while often uncomfortable, is essential. Especially in a field that holds such profound potential for impact.

Not long ago, early childhood was often seen as preparation for "real learning" that would come later. But as I have grown in this field, alongside the field itself, I have witnessed a quiet but powerful shift.

We now know that the earliest years aren't a rehearsal; they are the main stage. Every glance, gesture, conversation, and connection is laying the groundwork for how children see themselves and engage with the world. The science confirms what many of us have long felt in our hearts: these moments matter. And with that knowledge comes a responsibility, not just to care, but to be intentional about the culture we create, the relationships we nurture, and the possibilities we imagine together.

As our understanding evolves, so must our systems. The science is clear: what happens in the early years lays the foundation for everything that follows. Let's meet that truth with action by embracing innovation, centering relationships, and creating early childhood environments that reflect both the tenderness and the transformative power of these foundational years.

Insights in Practice
Shifting Staff Culture from Compliance to Connection

AI-Inspired Questions

In my program, are staff meetings spaces for compliance or for connection, collaboration, and growth?

How can I bring more curiosity and appreciation into my next conversation, even if it's a hard one?

Reflective Exercise

Meeting Reframe: Look at the agenda for your next staff meeting. Circle the compliance-based items (e.g., reminders, checklists, updates). Then, reframe at least one of them into a connection-based discussion. For example: instead of "new sick policy updates," ask, "What strategies have helped you manage sick days while supporting your team and families?" Notice how the tone of the meeting shifts.

Practice Tip

Begin your next team meeting with a "What Went Well?" round. Invite each staff member to share one positive moment from their week. This simple shift sets a tone of appreciation, highlights strengths, and builds trust. Over time, this practice turns meetings from dreaded tasks into spaces people actually look forward to.

Chapter Eight

WHAT LIFTS US UP?

"WHAT WE DO IN THE FIRST FEW YEARS OF LIFE WILL HAVE EVERYTHING TO DO WITH A PERSON'S NEXT 85."

-Eleanor Roosevelt

If you asked a team of early childhood educators what low morale looks like in their program or school, they would have a detailed and emotionally charged list: everything that isn't working, who should be blamed, and how the problems could be "fixed" followed by an even deeper sense of frustration and fatigue. The widespread acceptance of that mindset stems from very real and longstanding systemic challenges.

Despite their expertise, passion, and the immense responsibility of caring for children in their most formative years, early childhood educators are often underpaid, under-resourced, and undervalued compared to K–12 and higher education professionals. The science of brain development tells us that early childhood is a critical window for learning and relational growth, but our systems have been slow to reflect that truth in funding, policies, and professional respect.

Understandably, morale is low. The job is complex, emotional, and misunderstood. It demands that educators hold the emotions of not only young children but also of families, coworkers, and even entire communities, all while pushing through exhaustion, limited resources, and high expectations.

And yet, hope remains.

Holding Both: Mindset and Advocacy

Throughout this book, you' have seen an emphasis on mindset, not as a bandage or bypass for real challenges, but as a foundation for meaningful and lasting change. Appreciative Inquiry is not about ignoring problems. It's about changing how we engage with them. It invites us to ask: What's working?, What gives life to our profession?, Where have we been strong before?, and How can we build from that strength now?

Some might hear this and think it places the burden of change solely on individual educators. That's not the intent, nor the full truth. A strengths-based mindset doesn't replace advocacy for systemic change, it fuels it. When we see ourselves and one another as capable, connected, and worthy of joy, we're more likely to stay in the work long enough to change the conditions that make it so hard.

We can hold both the need for internal reflection and the call for external action.

We can honor our exhaustion and still imagine better systems.

We can acknowledge that morale is low because the job is undervalued and still choose to celebrate what makes the work beautiful, worthy, and full of possibility.

The TRF offers a bridge between the personal and the systemic. When we focus on what applies to educators' lived realities, when we nurture relationships that sustain and strengthen us, and when we create space for honest reflection, we cultivate not only resilience, but readiness for change. That readiness fuels powerful collective advocacy.

Educators are not broken. The system is. But together, grounded in strengths and guided by vision, we can reshape the story and the structure of early childhood education.

What if instead of only naming what's broken, we noticed what's possible? This shift doesn't ignore the very real challenges, it invites us to approach them differently.

That's the heart of this work, holding both the seriousness of our challenges and the lightness that keeps us going. While we push for systemic change and nurture a mindset of resilience, we also need ways to sustain ourselves in the every day. Sometimes, what restores us isn't another meeting or training. It's a moment of silliness, creativity, or small success that reminds us we're human.

That's where Goodifying, possiblitizing and creating O'playsis comes in.

Dr. Godwin's idea of being a "possibilizer" sparked something in me: a reminder that our mindset shapes our experience. By expanding our language to include playful, hopeful terms like "goodify" and "o'playsis" from the Life is Good Playmaker Project, we can see everyday moments through a lens of growth, creativity, and potential. These small shifts, like turning a chore into a game or reframing "I have to" into "I get to" offer us tools to navigate the hard stuff without losing sight of what's still good.

Goodifying is improving a task, game, or anything that can feel like a chore. For me, that looks like seeing if I can get a task done before my toast is done. I may run upstairs to grab the laundry and throw in a load before the toaster pops.

An O'Playsis isn't found on a map. It's sparked by sidewalk chalk, blanket forts, or a spontaneous dance party. It's the magical place where curiosity, connection, and imagination meet. In an O'Playsis, adults get to be kids again, and kids remind us how to live. It's less about where you are, and more about how you feel when you're there.

While an O'Playsis may be playful and imaginative, its impact is anything but trivial. These uplifting moments underscore the importance of levity amidst serious work. presence, and celebration.

That same spirit is at the heart of Appreciative Inquiry. Whether we are engaging with children or collaborating with colleagues, this mindset helps us tune into the moments of success and connection that often go unnoticed. And just like an O'Playsis, Appreciative Inquiry creates a sense of belonging and possibility, not by denying reality, but by choosing where to place our attention.

In Appreciative Inquiry, human growth is most powerful when we focus on strengths. In parenting and teaching, this means noticing and affirming what's going well. When a child offers a toy to a friend, we do not just move on. We pause, name the kindness, and let them know how much their thoughtfulness matters. In the workplace, the same principle applies: recognizing when a colleague navigates a tough parent conversation or comes up with a creative scheduling solution builds trust, motivation, and a sense of shared purpose.

Equally important is understanding our own emotional landscape. Embracing both positive and difficult emotions helps us respond with intention instead of reaction. It's okay to feel sad, angry, or overwhelmed. Those feelings are valid and welcome. Acknowledging them, rather than brushing them aside, supports long-term well-being. When we frame challenges as opportunities for learning rather than evidence of failure, we shift from self-criticism to self-compassion. Practicing mindfulness, observing our thoughts and feelings without judgment grounds us in the present and gives us a clearer, more balanced view of our experiences.

This mindset helps us reframe both small moments and larger narratives. When a child says, "I am not good at this," we can respond, "You have not learned that, yet." opens the door to innovation. These are the moments where Appreciative Inquiry shines, when we choose to ask, What is working and what is possible?

"What people need is encouragement. Their natural resisting powers should be strengthened, not weakened. Instead of always harping on a person's faults, tell them of their virtues.

Try to pull them out of their rut. Hold up to them their best self, their real self that can dare and do and win! People radiate what is in their minds and their hearts." -Eleanor H. Porter

It's important to distinguish authentic positivity from toxic positivity. Eleanor H. Porter's beloved character Pollyanna, introduced in her 1913 novel, has long been misunderstood. While some have dismissed her as naïve or cheerful, her "glad game" was never about ignoring hardship. The choice was to confront hardship with hope. Even in moments of deep adversity, Pollyanna found something to hold on to, a truth, a strength, a reason to keep going. That kind of resilience is not superficial; it's powerful.

Appreciative inquiry shares that same nuance. It doesn't avoid the hard stuff; it honors it and asks, "What else is true?" It allows us to acknowledge grief, frustration, or fear while still leaving space for possibility, purpose, and connection. That balance between realism and optimism is a powerful act of leadership, at home, at work, and within ourselves.

In early childhood education, we apply this every day. We validate children's feelings while nurturing their capacity to persevere: "I know you're sad, and this feeling won't last forever." In teaching, we reflect on what's working, especially when things feel tough and let those strengths guide our next steps. We name challenges directly, then invite co-creation of solutions through strengths-based questions. We allow space for grief and fatigue and, when ready, shift our focus to what's working, what brings us joy, and what we can do next.

This is the connective tissue where gratitude, a growth mindset, and positive psychology intersect with Appreciative Inquiry and workplace culture. It's not about sugarcoating reality but about shaping our perspective to foster resilience and well-being. Dr. Robert Emmons' research on gratitude shows us how this practice can transform how we move through our days, increasing optimism and lowering entitlement and burnout. Gratitude acts as a powerful counter to the toxic elements of work culture, creating environments where people feel valued and motivated rather than drained and blamed. (Emmons, 2017)

Researchers have conducted extensive studies on positive education in elementary and higher education. In considering the traditional academic goals of schools alongside character development, did researchers make a mistake in identifying where foundational social and emotional skills are learned? Research shows most brain development (90%) happens before age five.

In early childhood education (ECE), a positive approach integrates positive psychology principles, fostering well-being, resilience, and character strengths into young children's developmental experiences.

Understanding these matters, especially for those of us who grew up in cultures that emphasized constant problem-solving, finger-pointing, and the glorification of overworking. Many of us witnessed firsthand how this robbed our families of balance, neglected mental health, and perpetuated stress across generations. By rooting our work in genuine appreciation, curiosity, and collective strength, we can break these cycles, modeling for children and colleagues alike what it means to live and work in ways that honor both reality and hope.

This philosophy harmonizes with the mission of the International Positive Education Network (IPEN), which unites a worldwide community of educators, researchers, policymakers, and practitioners dedicated to the idea that education should cultivate not only academic achievement but also character, well-being, and essential life skills. Their work advances the global Positive Education Movement, which seeks to embed the principles of positive psychology into education systems around the world, supporting student flourishing while nurturing resilient, well-supported educators.

Globally, this trend reflects Appreciative Inquiry and strengths-based teaching in all areas of education, including early childhood education. It emphasizes that learning environments must be both rigorous and relational, helping children and adults alike grow through connection, curiosity, and a shared commitment to what's possible.

Side note: The International Positive Education Network (IPEN) uses the term "rigorous" to emphasize that Positive Education is not about lowering academic expectations or replacing core learning with feel-good activities. Instead, it means combining high standards for academic excellence with an equally strong commitment to nurturing well-being, character, and life skills. (The International Positive Education Network, 2025)

The Positive Education Movement's Guiding Principles:

+ Well-being matters just as much as academics.

+ Schools should cultivate strengths, not just fix weaknesses.

+ We can teach and model emotional intelligence, resilience, empathy, and optimism.

+ Teachers and leaders need to experience well-being themselves to foster it in others

+ Education should empower students to flourish, not just perform

Positive Education in Action:

+ We integrate social-emotional learning (SEL) throughout the curriculum.

+ Classroom activities could include gratitude journaling, mindfulness techniques, and exercises to identify students' strengths.

+ Positive psychology training and well-being initiatives for staff.

+ School cultures should prioritize a sense of belonging, growth, and purpose.

+ A strengths-based approach to collaborating with parents and families.

IPEN mainly serves K–12 and higher education, but its core principles are also relevant to early childhood education. In Early Childhood Education (ECE), a key principle has always been whole-child development, nurturing children's social, emotional, and cognitive skills together. The principles of positive psychology support the strength-based, relationship-focused approaches common in a good deal of early childhood education programs.

Investing in teacher well-being, as much as teaching methods, shows that happy teachers create better classrooms. Optimizing well-being across a lifetime requires nurturing optimism, emotional regulation, and positive relationships, which are best cultivated during the formative early years.

Creating a Balance

My past ownership of an early childhood education program brought a vivid and powerful memory of my father's demanding career at IBM during the 1970s and 80s. I was forced to reflect upon specific methods and strategies he used to overcome the considerable challenges he faced while building a successful professional life during that dynamic period of technological advancement and corporate transformation.

I thought that the distribution of my time between professional duties and personal pursuits was an equitable arrangement, a state I perceived as work-life balance; it looked like filling every bit of spare time with more things to do; that would advance me somehow, right? If your schedule isn't overwhelmingly full, could that suggest that you haven't been taking on a sufficient workload or are not dedicating yourself to enough tasks?

Throughout my childhood, watching my parents, the subject of balance was never a discussion. My dad's methods of stress management was comprised of smoking an excessive number of cigarettes, coffee, and an unhealthy devotion to long work hours. This perspective is what I adopted in my adult life, minus the cigarettes. It has taken me well into adulthood to learn that the business will not dissolve if I don't work until midnight.

However, my parents instilled in me the importance of hard work, a value I have carried forward and thank them for. The emphasis on workplace wellness, mental health, and balance in today's businesses leads me to believe that future generations will finally grasp the concept of work balance. Work-life balance is not a thing. We get one life and it should not be something that is balanced with work.

I spoke with a group of individuals whose demanding jobs at a state government agency leave them short on time and staff and with mountains of work. The division's professionals address the diverse needs of children, encompassing those in foster care, those with behavioral challenges, and those with special needs. "It's all great, and I understand," one person said at the close of our basic AI overview, "but honestly, I am buried in paperwork and can barely breathe. I am struggling to believe that it would be possible for me to alter my way of thinking and approach to life."

I acknowledged that the constant barrage of emails can be overwhelming and that it's easy to get bogged down in the daily grind of responding to them. I replied, "Yes, I understand your perspective, AND I want you to know I am listening. To simplify and focus on a single accomplishment from today, we can highlight either clearing your inbox of emails or taking part in five meetings, representing productive achievements." It is so easy to become overwhelmed by the sheer volume of tasks we must complete, especially when we don't have enough time to do them all. To simplify the process, try to pinpoint a single successful event or task from each half of the day, the morning and the afternoon.

Research suggests that genetic factors may contribute to an individual's tendency toward optimism (Plomin et al., 1992). Inherent optimism isn't required. You can still be optimistic even if you are genetically prone to pessimism.

Reframing negative experiences and practicing gratitude can foster learned optimism, as highlighted in Seligman's (2006) research. In later research (Taylor et al., 2004), it was found that a strong support system leads to more optimistic thinking through increased security and encouragement. The chance for self-improvement helps people stay hopeful. According to studies, mindfulness, goal-setting, and kindness boost optimism by fostering a sense of purpose and control (Lyubomirsky, 2007). In the end, some people may have a natural inclination for it, but through intentional habits, supportive relationships, and a growth-oriented mindset, one can cultivate the skill of leaning toward optimism.

Dr. Carol Dweck, a psychologist with a Ph.D. from Yale, is best known for her groundbreaking work on motivation, self-concept, and the impact of beliefs on learning and achievement. Her influential mindset theory explores how individuals' beliefs about intelligence and ability shape their behavior. Her research shows that people with a growth mindset (those who believe that abilities can be developed through effort and learning) are more likely to embrace challenges and persist through setbacks. In contrast, those with a fixed mindset, who see abilities as static or unchangeable, avoid challenges and give up more easily.

Dweck's work aligns with the principles of Appreciative Inquiry (AI). Both frameworks take a strengths-based, forward-looking approach to growth, whether in individuals or organizations. While Dweck emphasizes the development of abilities through encouragement, effort, and constructive feedback; Appreciative Inquiry focuses on identifying and amplifying strengths to drive meaningful change. In both models, language plays a powerful role. AI uses generative, strengths-based questions to inspire action, much like Dweck's research shows how process-oriented praise fosters motivation, resilience, and deeper engagement.

Together, these approaches support a culture of continuous learning, adaptability, and possibility where challenges are not obstacles but invitations to grow.

Early Childhood Applications

Using positive language and affirmation helps children develop emotional resilience while also providing validation for the complex emotions that are often a normal part of childhood. Learning and adapting throughout adulthood is a valuable skill, which shows capacity. Small wins are the fuel that drives progress forward; they are essential building blocks for more significant achievements. Foster a culture of continuous learning and resilience.

Individuals with a growth mindset, believing they can develop their talents and capabilities, show greater motivation and perseverance, achieving lasting success. Embracing a growth mindset changes the approach of individuals and organizations, placing the ongoing pursuit of learning and development above the often-limiting goal of perfection; this shift fosters supportive and collaborative settings conducive to growth and success. By providing resources and guidance, we empower children and adults alike to challenge the fixed mindset and cultivate a belief in their ability to learn and grow, leading to success and fulfillment.

Whenever a child says, "I can't pour the water without spilling," it's often a cue, not just of frustration, but of a developing skill that needs support. Rather than stepping in to do it for them, we might say, "You're still learning how to pour carefully. Let's try again together. "

This gentle reframe communicates that learning is a process, not a fixed ability. It offers emotional support while still encouraging independence and persistence. Saying "you can't do it yet" turns a moment of struggle into a chance to build confidence, resilience, and trust in the adult-child relationship.

The power of yet was something my elementary school self needed. Since the fourth grade, I insisted to myself and everyone around me that mathematics was a subject I could not understand. "I have never been good at this and never will be."

A low grade on a test felt like confirmation of what I already feared: "See? I knew I wasn't smart enough for this." Discouraged, I stopped trying, believing that more effort wouldn't make a difference. Instead of seeking help or studying harder, I withdrew, convinced my abilities were fixed and unchangeable. This fixed mindset blinded me to the possibility that intelligence and skills can grow with practice, support, and persistence.

Looking back, I can see how that belief created a self-fulfilling prophecy. By assuming I couldn't improve, I stopped engaging in the very actions that might have helped me succeed. Had I approached the challenge with a growth mindset, I might have seen my struggles in math and test-taking not as evidence of failure, but as opportunities to stretch and grow. Instead, I resigned myself to my perceived limitations and in doing so, held myself back.

That experience became a powerful turning point, one I did not understand until much later. It taught me how deeply our beliefs can shape our behaviors, and how easily a fixed mindset can trap us in a cycle of self-doubt and missed opportunities. But it also planted the seed for something greater: the realization that change is possible, and that mindset is one of our most powerful tools. I'll share more soon about how that early self-fulfilling prophecy led me to the work I do now and how I eventually rewrote the story I once believed about myself.

Insights in Practice
From Low Morale to Possibility and Connection

**AI-Inspired
Questions**

When morale feels low, what strengths in myself, my team, or my community can I choose to notice and nurture?

What possibilities exist if I shift from asking "what's wrong" to "what's working and what's next?"

**Reflective
Exercise**

Goodify It: Identify one task this week that usually feels draining (e.g., documentation, cleanup, or an end-of-day routine). Reframe it with a playful or meaningful twist, set a timer, add music, or turn it into a team challenge. At the end of the week, jot down how this shift impacted your mood or energy.

**Practice
Tip**

Try creating an "O'Playsis" moment at work. This could be as simple as sharing sidewalk chalk with children, starting a staff meeting with a silly question, or bringing in a playful ritual like a gratitude high-five. Notice how small, intentional moments of levity build resilience, connection, and joy.

Chapter Nine

STRENGTHS AT THE CENTER

"SOMETIMES WE FEEL STUCK IN CIRCUMSTANCES WE CANNOT CHANGE OR CONTROL, LIKE COMPENSATION. WE ALSO HAVE TO RECOGNIZE THAT WE HAVE STRENGTHS THAT WE CAN PRESERVE. AND IF WE GLEANED THE BEST FROM THE PRACTITIONERS ALL AROUND US AND ANCHOR OUR WORK ON THE ESSENTIAL PRINCIPLES THAT GUIDE CHANGE, WE CAN BE ARCHITECTS OF THAT CHANGE."

-Dr. Valora Washington (Washington, 2019)

Appreciative inquiry holds tremendous potential in early childhood education, offering a powerful framework for fostering positive change and meaningful growth. Across programs, its principles have inspired a range of impactful strategies that center on what's working, amplifying strengths rather than dwelling on deficits.

By focusing on children's abilities and potential, we nurture their confidence and help them meet challenges with resilience. This strengths-based lens also enhances professional practice. When directors and educators engage in Appreciative Inquiry conversations, they reflect on what's going well in their classrooms and explore strategies for continuous improvement. For instance, a preschool administrator might ask staff to recall moments when teaching felt especially energizing or impactful. What conditions made those moments possible? Sharing these stories often leads to collaborative learning and richer, more responsive teaching practices.

Beyond the classroom, this approach helps build a thriving educational community. Integrating Appreciative Inquiry into everyday interactions like parent-teacher conferences strengthens partnerships with families. A simple shift in language, such as asking, "What aspects of your child's learning bring you the most joy?" can move the conversation from evaluation to connection. It opens space for trust, shared insight, and celebration of each child's unique journey.

As we move forward, we'll explore specific ways these practices support well-being, connection, and a more empowered approach to education for children, families, and educators.

Large Scale Change

To elevate the early childhood education profession, the Power to the Profession initiative, led by NAEYC, brought together national organizations and diverse stakeholders to develop a shared vision for the field. The result was the Unifying Framework for the Early Childhood Education Profession, a powerful document outlining a collective commitment to advancing equity, compensation, professional preparation, and accountability across all roles and settings in early childhood.

What made this process unique was its foundation in Appreciative Inquiry (AI), a strengths-based, collaborative approach to organizational change. Rather than beginning with problems or deficits, AI asks generative questions like: "What's already working?" and "What do we want to grow more of?" Throughout the Power to the Profession process, NAEYC used AI to bring people together around shared values and aspirations instead of allowing differences to derail the work.

This approach created space for stakeholders, educators, higher education faculty, policy advocates, and system leaders to share their lived experiences and dream together about what the profession could become. The AI process included large-group summits, facilitated dialogue, and iterative feedback loops that allowed the collective vision to evolve. By focusing on strengths and engaging multiple perspectives, Appreciative Inquiry helped ensure that the Unifying Framework was not only inclusive and visionary, but also actionable. It honored the wisdom already present in the field and invited everyone to be part of shaping the future of early childhood education. To learn more about this, visit: https://www.naeyc.org/our-work/initiatives/profession

Multiple states adopted similar processes, echoing NAEYC's initiative in ways that honored local strengths and workforce voices. In Vermont, for example, a small but mighty group of early childhood advocates, many of whom had spent decades working in classrooms used Appreciative Inquiry to galvanize momentum for systemic change.

Vermont Birth to Five (which later became Let's Grow Kids) convened a statewide workgroup to explore how early childhood education could be more fully recognized as a profession. They began by "taking the temperature" of the field. Surveying a large cross-section of early educators to understand their hopes, fears, and readiness for change. This project, inspired by the AI-driven Power to the Profession initiative, invited Vermont's early childhood workforce not just to respond but to lead the conversation.

One of the most powerful set of voices in this effort came from a group of individuals from an organization called Let's Grow Kids, that saw the process through. They were key advocates whose leadership wasn't rooted in titles or hierarchy, it was rooted in mindset. They modeled what it looks like to approach systemic change through the lens of Appreciative Inquiry. They relentlessly focused on what was possible, grounded in a deep belief in the field's wisdom and potential. The clarity, optimism, and ability to listen deeply created a ripple effect: this helped others see themselves as change agents, too.

This is where the connection between individual mindset and collective transformation becomes clear. The inner work of developing a strengths-based mindset, believing in shared possibility, and staying rooted in relationship laid the foundation for outer work like policy shifts, funding reforms, and professional recognition. These were not separate journeys, but parallel ones.

The Vermont initiative ultimately contributed to meaningful changes in public perception, workforce development, and state-level investments in early childhood education. To learn more about the scope and evolution of this project, visit: https://www.vtaeyc.org/the-ece-profession/

As we move forward, these stories remind us that meaningful systems change begins with people who believe change is possible and who commit to doing the reflective, relational work it requires. Appreciative Inquiry gives us the mindset and method to build that kind of movement: one that starts from within and grows outward, lifting not just individuals but entire communities.

What does a coffee company have to do with early childhood programs? No one wants to see what happens in a classroom without it!

In all seriousness.....

The impact of Bob Stiller, founder of Keurig Green Mountain and author of the book "Better and Better: Creating a Culture of Purpose, Excellence, and Transformative Human Engagement," is undeniable. (Stiller, 2024)

In the early 2000s, Green Mountain Coffee Roasters was expanding, but Stiller noticed a disconnect: while profits were increasing, internal communication and engagement were not keeping pace. He recognized that something was missing in the culture, a deeper connection to purpose, people, and shared vision.

Stiller embraced Appreciative Inquiry to reimagine leadership and organizational development. Rather than focusing on problems and deficits, AI encouraged the company to explore: What's already working well? When are we at our best? What do we want more of?

Through company-wide AI summits, Green Mountain employees across departments and levels came together to dream, design, and co-create the future of the company. Team members felt seen, valued, and heard, leading to more open communication and collaboration. The company's social and environmental mission became central, not just a marketing point, but part of everyday decision-making. Stiller stepped back from traditional command-and-control leadership and leaned into co-creation, inviting others to lead from where they were.

Green Mountain Coffee became widely recognized not only for its business success but for its people-first, purpose-centered culture. AI helped create a workplace where people felt empowered, and that energy carried into the company's innovations, partnerships, and social impact work.

Bob Stiller's journey with Appreciative Inquiry illustrates how a shift in perspective, from deficit to possibility, can fuel sustainable growth, deepen connection, and help leaders evolve alongside their organizations. His story is a reminder that meaningful change starts with curiosity, trust, and a willingness to ask better questions.

Early childhood educators can draw powerful lessons from Bob Stiller's Appreciative Inquiry journey because while his story unfolded in the coffee industry, the principles he embraced resonate with the work of education, leadership, and care.

What Can Early Childhood Educators Learn from Bob Stiller?

Instead of asking "What's wrong?" Stiller began asking, "When are we at our best?"

This shift helped his team see what was already working and how to grow from there. Educators can apply this by asking children, families, and colleagues about strengths and successes, not just challenges.

Stiller moved away from top-down decision-making and invited his entire organization into visioning and planning. In early childhood, this reinforces that teachers, aides, and family partners all have valuable insights. Inviting them into decision-making increases buy-in and innovation.

When Green Mountain centered on its environmental and social mission, employees felt more connected to their work. In early childhood, reminding ourselves why we do this work shaping human potential can reignite motivation and joy.

Appreciative Inquiry helped Stiller focus on assets instead of constantly trying to fix weaknesses. For ECE professionals, this means focusing on children's strengths, educator talents, and what's working in your learning environment, not just the problems.

Stiller did not "fix" his company. He got curious about it. He created space for voices, stories, and shared dreaming. Educators can create a similar space in staff meetings, family partnerships, and even circle time, by listening more than directing.

Bob Stiller teaches us that leadership isn't about having all the answers, it's about creating space for shared discovery. Early childhood educators, by nature, are relationship builders, nurturers, and vision holders. By leaning into Appreciative Inquiry, they can deepen those strengths, building teams, classrooms, and communities that lead with joy, trust, and possibility.

Insights in Practice
Appreciative Inquiry in Classrooms,
Communities, and Systems

**AI-Inspired
Questions**

When my program, school, or team is at its
best, what does that look and feel like?

What strengths in my classroom or
organization could be amplified to create
even greater impact?

How might I invite families, colleagues, or
partners to co-create a vision of what's
possible?

**Reflective
Exercise**

Story Swap: At your next team meeting, ask
each person to share a short story about a
moment when teaching felt especially
energizing, joyful, or impactful. Then
discuss: What made those moments
possible? How can we create more of them
together?

Borrow Bob Stiller's approach: instead of beginning a conversation with "What's wrong?" begin with "When have we been at our best?"

Practice Tip

With families: "What brings your child the most joy in learning?"

With staff: "What's a recent moment that reminded you why you love this work?"

With policymakers or board members: "When have you seen early childhood programs make their strongest impact?"

Chapter Ten

INFUSING STRENGTHS INTO EVERYDAY PRACTICE

"CHILDREN'S PLAY IS NOT JUST KIDS' STUFF. CHILDREN'S PLAY IS RATHER THE STUFF OF MOST FUTURE INVENTIONS."

-Fred Rogers

We use various methods to achieve our goals and articulate our points. These include coordinating with prospective families, conducting tours, employee interviews, parent-teacher conferences, and interacting with children of diverse developmental levels while managing our personal lives.

I sought the perspectives and experiences of my colleagues with children in the early childhood age range regarding parent-teacher conferences.

The experiences ran the gamut.

One mother recounted that upon meeting with her three-year-old daughter's teacher after they had sat down, the teacher reported that her daughter was thriving and inquired if the parents had questions regarding her progress. The mother's eyes scanned the room, searching for materials the teacher might share, such as samples of emergent writing or assessment tools to help her better understand her child's abilities. Disappointed by an underwhelming experience, she and her partner reflected on their anticipation for the event, hoping to learn about their daughter's playmates, developmental milestones, and opportunities for engaging in activities at home. The duration of the conference was brief, concluding within a mere two minutes.

My memories of attending conferences for my children are a mixture of warm, exciting experiences and others that left me feeling defeated, not just as a parent but also for my child, who was struggling to develop a particular skill. Faced with adversity and challenges, when things are not going as planned or working correctly, it is easy to lose sight of what truly matters and what is essential. To complete the missing information, parents must create their own narrative educated guesses and assumptions.

Teachers should engage in a period of self-reflection focused on the individual academic growth of each student under their care to prepare for upcoming conferences.

Here is how a teacher may start the conversation.

Thank you both so much for taking the time to meet with me today. I cherish your partnership in supporting Nora's growth. Over the past several months, I have had the joy of observing Nora's strengths unfold in so many meaningful ways. One of the most beautiful things I have noticed is the close, playful connection she shares with her friend Jo. They often engage in imaginative play around shared interests, especially rainbows, unicorns, and mermaids, which reflect Nora's vibrant creativity and strong sense of friendship. She turns to her trusted peers for support during times of uncertainty, showing how attuned she is to relationships and emotional connection.

One particular moment stood out to me. About a month ago, when Nora approached me with feelings of frustration. Rather than reacting impulsively, she paused with me to take some deep breaths, which allowed us both to regulate and explore what was beneath her big emotions. While I can't recall the exact reason for her frustration, what stayed with me was her ability to pause, breathe, and reflect, a remarkable step in developing emotional awareness and self-regulation. Since then,

I have noticed Nora using deep breaths at other times when she's advocating for herself, which is a skill we know takes both courage and practice.

Another area where Nora continues to shine is in her physical confidence and determination. She's been working on mastering the slack line, returning to it again and again with focus and perseverance. Watching her push through each attempt and celebrate small wins along the way has been inspiring. It's clear that her belief in herself is growing, and it's a privilege to witness her learning that effort leads to progress.

What are some things you've noticed Nora doing at home that make you feel proud or show her growing confidence?"

In the Appreciative Inquiry framework, questions that generate positive energy and progress are considered life-giving. They spark reflection, uncover strengths, and invite possibility. During parent-teacher conferences, using these types of questions can steer the conversation from reporting on a child's performance to understanding their growth, character, and potential.

Using the TRF can transform parent-teacher conferences into meaningful, strengths-based conversations that build trust and deepen collaboration. Start by grounding the conversation in Relevance: focus on what matters most to the family and the child. This means highlighting specific examples of the child's growth, interests, and learning moments that connect directly to the family's values or goals. Next, center Relationship by creating an atmosphere of mutual respect and partnership. Begin with warmth, ask open-ended questions, and listen actively to families' insights, honoring their unique perspectives and expertise. Finally, invite Reflection by creating space for shared thinking about the child's development, challenges, and next steps. Ask questions like, "What's been going well at home?" or "What would you like us to work on together?" When used intentionally, the TRF ensures that conferences are not just check-ins, but collaborative experiences that empower families and educators alike to support the whole child.

Using the Triple R Framework as a guide for conferences, we can ask:

Relevance
+ What interests or skills has your child been most enthusiastic about lately?

+ Are there any new challenges or changes at home that we should know to best support your child?

+ What are your priorities for your child's learning and well-being this season?

+ Is there anything you wish we focused on more in the classroom right now?

Relationship
+ How does your child talk about school at home?

+ How can we strengthen the partnership between school and home?

+ What helps your child feel safe, connected, and confident in new or challenging situations?

+ Are there family traditions, values, or cultural practices you'd like us to incorporate or respect more fully?

Reflection
+ Since the start of the year, what growth or changes have you noticed in your child?

+ How do you feel your child's needs are being met, and where could we improve?

+ What questions or concerns do you have about your child's learning or social experiences?

+ What hopes do you have for your child's next steps, both academically and emotionally?

When teachers plan questions that invite parents to share stories of pride, joy, and resilience, they unlock deeper insights into the child's identity and learning beyond the classroom. This method not only reveals rich information, it also honors the parent's role as an expert on their child. Life-giving questions help build trust, strengthen the family-school partnership, and create a shared vision for the child's success rooted in strengths, curiosity, and connection.

Heartfelt appreciation forms the basis of these relationships; I picture it engraved on a heart, in contrast to the intellectual pursuit ("inquiry") I visualize inscribed on the brain.

Tours with Families

For many years, a family's first impression of a program began over the phone. That initial conversation offered a glimpse into the heart of the program. Professionalism paired with genuine warmth could be felt through tone alone, offering families comfort and reassurance. It's an emotional decision, especially when it marks a family's first time separating from their baby.

Today, in a world shaped by technology, families often rely on email, messaging apps, and social media to communicate, research, and connect with programs and other parents. While the tools have changed, the core questions remain the same: Will my child be safe? Will someone snuggle up and love them when I'm not there? These are the questions that live beneath every inquiry, and it's our job to ensure the answer is felt in every interaction, digital or otherwise.

By employing Appreciative Inquiry in family tours, early childhood programs can create a welcoming environment that emphasizes their finest qualities and cultivates a positive bond with prospective families, enhancing the overall experience for everyone involved. In contrast to the family tours that dwell on administrative details and logistical information, an AI-powered tour highlights the program's exceptional qualities, focusing on its strengths, past successes, and the distinctive features that set its learning environment apart.

Imagine a tour of a potential school that focuses on absences because of illness, tardiness policies, classroom management, and prohibited behaviors. It would be a real drag.

Begin each tour with a warm, enthusiastic welcome, setting the tone for an open and supportive environment where families feel safe sharing their hopes, concerns, and priorities. It's important to remember that families come with varied experiences, and their understanding of early childhood education is often shaped by their lived experiences. Whether through their own upbringing, stories from friends and family, or general life experience, these prior beliefs, while valid, may not encompass the full scope of what high-quality early education offers. Each tour becomes a powerful opportunity to expand perspectives, inviting families to discover the thoughtful, research-based practices that help children grow.

For instance, when a two-year-old makes marks on paper with crayons or pencils, it may look like simple play. In reality, they are developing fine motor skills, strengthening hand-eye coordination, and expressing creativity, all foundational to later learning. By encouraging families to ask questions and explore the "why" behind what they see, we help shift the focus from uncertainty to curiosity, from fear to possibility. It's in these moments that families reimagine what's possible for their child's development and for their own role in that journey.

During the tour, families can be invited to explore the program and experience its joyful, engaging nature firsthand.

The director can emphasize the rich, collaborative projects started by students and the thoughtful use of open-ended questioning by educators, both of which reflect a deep commitment to student-centered, inquiry-driven learning.

This innovative approach sparks meaningful conversations, encourages creative thinking, and nurtures children's natural curiosity, resulting in more authentic problem-solving and a strong foundation for lifelong learning.

The tour can offer families a transparent, detailed view of the program's environment, curriculum, and culture.

Questions like, "What kind of learning experiences do you hope your child will have?" help bridge families' aspirations with the opportunities available in the program.

By the end of the tour, families are invited into a collaborative conversation to identify meaningful milestones and set shared goals, establishing a foundation of trust and mutual respect. While families hold the power to choose what's best for their child, the program honors them as experts in their child's journey, and uses an Appreciative Inquiry lens to foster a welcoming, confidence-building environment. This approach ensures alignment between the program's strengths-based philosophy and the family's vision for their child's early learning experience.

Strengths-based interview for prospective employees

A strengths-based interview shifts the spotlight toward a candidate's natural talents and aptitudes, exploring how they've used those strengths in previous roles to achieve meaningful results. Rather than focusing on shortcomings, this approach emphasizes what individuals do well, creating a more empowering, respectful, and authentic dialogue. It fosters trust and openness, allowing candidates to reflect on their motivations, clarify their areas of expertise, and articulate how their strengths align with the role.

This process is not just about evaluating experience; it's about discovering alignment, highlighting the connection between what the candidate brings and what the program needs. By focusing on strengths and successes, interviewers gain a clearer, more holistic picture of a candidate's potential. This leads to well-informed hiring decisions, strengthens team dynamics, and contributes to a values-aligned match between the candidate and the organization's mission and culture.

See end of the book for template and question suggestions.

Insights in Practice
Applying Appreciative Inquiry to Everyday Interactions

**AI-Inspired
Questions**

What questions can I ask in parent-teacher conferences that highlight strengths and possibilities instead of just progress reports?

How can I help prospective families and employees see what makes our program come alive?

**Reflective
Exercise**

Rewrite the Question: Take one "standard" question you might use in a conference, tour, or interview (e.g., "What concerns do you have?"). Reframe it into an appreciative version (e.g., "What aspects of your child's learning bring you the most joy?" or "What strengths do you hope to bring to this role?"). Try this out in practice and note how the energy of the conversation changes.

Use the Triple R Framework™ (Relevance, Relationship, Reflection) in your next interaction:

> + Relevance: Start with what matters most to the child, family, or candidate.

Practice Tip

> + Relationship: Create a warm, collaborative atmosphere where voices are heard and valued.

> + Reflection: Invite shared insights and co-create next steps.

This simple structure can turn everyday moments into meaningful, strengths-based conversations that build trust and connection.

Chapter Eleven

START WITH HUMANITY: LIVING THE QUESTIONS

"I AM BECAUSE WE ARE."

-Ubuntu proverb (widely cited by Desmond Tutu)

How do you live into the principles of Appreciative Inquiry?

I met Dr. Patrick Makokoro in Hawaii when we were both part of the same global leader cohort for the World Forum Foundation for Early Care and Education. Meeting people worldwide and working toward a common goal is a powerful opportunity. The goal is to improve the world for children and families. The relationships formed at the World Forum have stood the test of time.

Dr. Patrick Makokoro is a Zimbabwean-born social entrepreneur, educator, and community development practitioner renowned for his application of Appreciative Inquiry (AI) in early childhood development (ECD) and community empowerment across Africa. As an ardent AI practitioner, he emphasizes strength-based approaches over deficit-focused models when co-creating strategies with individuals, organizations, and communities.

Reuniting with people like Patrick through our work has been a gift. We met up in China, where I could give him a copy of my first book that he wrote a testimonial for that landed on the back cover.

A few years later, attending the World Forum in Panama, I had the pleasure of introducing him to my friend Alyssa whom I have mentioned throughout the book.

I was eager for these two powerhouses to connect.

Fast-forward to 2024, when Alyssa and Patrick met at a UNESCO summit in Paris, France, where they sat on a panel of experts together. My two favorites appeared together onstage.

This connection led to Patrick being a guest on Alyssa's podcast, Voices of Your Village, showcasing his commitment to Appreciative Inquiry through a strength-based design philosophy that underpins his innovation and growth, which I found remarkable.

"The longer I do this work, the more I return to one essential truth: real change begins in the way we see each other and in the questions we choose to ask." That truth echoed clearly for me as I listened to the conversation between Patrick and Alyssa, where they reflected on what it means to create inclusive, life-giving spaces.

One phrase stayed with me: "I want to be part of a world where we ask, not assume." That sentiment captures so much of what Appreciative Inquiry has taught me about leadership, relationships, and the culture we co-create when we choose curiosity over certainty.

Patrick's stories about raising children rooted in cultural pride, and his vision for classrooms where compassion and identity are honored, reminded me that the work of building belonging doesn't come from grand gestures, it grows through everyday moments of listening, noticing, and making room for one another's truths. The conversation wasn't about strategy; it was about humanity. And that is what gives life. (Campbell, 2025)

This book has been a collection of stories, ideas, and tools but, more than that, it's a call to stay grounded in what matters: relationships, reflection, and the belief that something better is always possible. Appreciative Inquiry doesn't offer all the answers; it offers better questions. And sometimes, one powerful question is all it takes to imagine more than we thought possible. Patrick's words reinforced what I believe through my work: that strengths-based change doesn't begin with a checklist. It begins with a mindset. One that values listening over labeling, presence over performance, and possibility over perfection. These conversations, along with countless others shared throughout this book, are reminders that the path forward is built not through fixing, but through asking, noticing, and appreciating what gives life together.

You don't need formal training to begin. You just need a willingness to wonder. A belief that growth is possible. A commitment to move forward, imperfectly, but together.

This kind of presence doesn't just support children's learning; it reshapes systems, reclaims hope, and reaffirms our shared humanity. When we lead with appreciation, we see each other differently, and we imagine a world that works better for all of us.

Conclusion: Living the Questions

As we close this book, I hope you're leaving with more than strategies or frameworks. I hope you're leaving with a renewed sense of possibility.

The work of early childhood education is not for the faint of heart. It asks us to be brave in the face of complexity, to remain curious even when we're exhausted, and to lead with love in systems that don't always make space for it. And yet, despite the messiness, the weight, and the quiet frustrations, this work is deeply meaningful. It shapes futures. It uplifts families. It creates communities of care.

Appreciative Inquiry reminds us to begin not with what's broken, but with what gives life. It's a practice of scrutinizing what's working and asking how we might grow more of it.

The TRF, Relevance, Relationship, and Reflection offers a way to anchor this mindset in our daily work, helping us stay grounded in what truly matters.

In these pages, you've seen how this approach can transform everything from staff meetings to mission statements, from classroom design to systems-level advocacy. But perhaps the most powerful transformations happen in quiet, everyday moments: a better question, a deeper breath, a decision to focus on strengths even in the middle of struggle.

My dear friend and global colleague, Patrick reminds us that change begins with humanity. In conversations about race, identity, and inclusion, Patrick urges us to bring compassion, curiosity, and courageous listening. These are the same principles at the heart of Appreciative Inquiry. When we start with relationship, when we honor each other's stories, and when we create space for shared dreaming, we don't just make our classrooms better, we reshape our communities.

This book is not the end of the conversation. It's an invitation.

+ An invitation to pause and notice what's working.

+ To ask bold, beautiful questions.

+ To lead with curiosity rather than fear.

+ To believe that change is not only possible, but already beginning.

So wherever you go from here, into your classroom, your program, your community, or your next big decision, I hope you'll carry this mindset with you. Not as pressure to be perfect, but as permission to keep practicing.

Because when you believe in what's possible, you create the conditions for others to believe, too.

Let that vision guide you. Let your questions lead. And most of all, let your belief in what's possible to be the thread that ties it all together.

Insights in Practice
Living the Questions

**AI-Inspired
Questions**

What gives life to my work, my classroom, or my community right now?

When have I seen humanity shine through in small, everyday ways?

What is one bold, beautiful question I can carry into my next conversation?

**Reflective
Exercise**

Belief in Possibility Journal: At the end of each week, jot down one moment when you felt hope or possibility in your work. It might be a child's smile, a breakthrough with a family, or a colleague's idea. Over time, notice how these "life-giving" moments create a map of resilience and meaning.

**Practice
Tip**

Start your next conversation, or personal reflection not with what's broken, but with: "What's working, and how can we grow more of it?"

Small shifts in language create big shifts in culture.

ACKNOWLEDGEMENTS

Mentors & Guides

Dr. Lindsey Godwin, you were the one who opened the door to Appreciative Inquiry for me, and nothing has looked the same since. Your brilliance, generosity, and unwavering belief in possibility have shaped not only this book, but the way I see the world. The seeds you planted in me years ago continue to grow in ways far beyond what I could have imagined, and I will always carry deep gratitude for the light you shine.

Dr. Matthew Moehle, thank you for reminding me that my story matters. When I felt stuck, you helped me return to my "why," and gave me the courage to keep going.

 EdLinks, your generous support and belief in this work helped bring these words to life.

Alyssa Blask Campbell—thank you for modeling integrity, curiosity, and vision. Our lives have become so deeply intertwined, and I am endlessly grateful for your honesty, brilliance, and steadfast support.

Mom and Dad, thank you for always reminding me I could do hard things, even when it took me longer to believe it.

Joseph, thank you for your perspective and for honoring the beauty of our shared story.

Leigh, your thoughtful edits and organized eye were gifts I did not have but deeply needed. And your words, "we write the same," will always be one of my favorite compliments.

Todd and my children (D, J, Z, M, J, and C), You fill my cup daily with your love, opinions, group texts, and advice I did not always ask for but usually needed. You have always been my "why" in early childhood education, and you always will be.

Laura Butler, thank you for lending your wisdom and feedback in your very first month of retirement. That gift meant more than you know. You will always be a guiding light in this journey. Alicia Barnachez and my Life Is Good Playmaker Project Family, thank you for reminding the world, again and again, that play is healing. Hannah Formella, thank you for your thoughtful eye, gentle edits, and cheering me on through messy drafts.

To the entire Seed & Sew team, words will never be enough. The connection, laughter, honesty, and heart we share in this work and with one another are rare and beautiful. I am endlessly grateful for each of you, exactly as you are.

Together, you have shown me that this work, this life, and this book could be so much **more than we imagined**.

Appendix A

These questions encourage collaboration and focus on building strengths within the early childhood education community.

+ What's taking shape in our early childhood program right now?

+ What are the good things you hear from the various perspectives children, families, and colleagues share?

+ What's emerging for you as we discuss the needs and goals of our classroom or program?

+ What new connections are you making between children's experiences, your teaching practices, and our shared vision?

+ What had real meaning for you from what you've observed or heard from the children or families?

+ What surprised you about the children's responses, interactions, or learning processes?

+ What challenged your thinking or assumptions about how we approach teaching and learning?

+ What's missing from this picture of our early childhood environment or curriculum so far?

+ What might we not see about the children's experiences or our program's impact?

+ What areas need more clarity or understanding regarding child development or family engagement?

+ What has been your recent central learning, insight, or discovery from working with children or colleagues?

+ What's the next level of thinking we must do to enhance the children's experiences and outcomes?

Creating change and engagement in your early childhood program. Envisioning the future.

+ What would creating meaningful change in supporting children's learning and development take?

+ What could make us feel engaged and energized about our work with young children?

+ What's possible here, and who cares deeply about making it happen? What's possible here, and who cares intensely about making it happen?

+ What bold and innovative ideas could we explore if we completely guaranteed our success?

+ What needs our immediate attention as we move forward to improve our program or practices?

+ What conversation, if we began it today, could ripple out to create new opportunities for the future of early childhood education?

+ How can we best support each other in taking the next steps toward our shared goals?

+ What unique contributions can each of us make to strengthen our team and enhance children's experiences?

+ What resources, skills, or relationships can help us navigate potential roadblocks?

+ What small, impactful action could we take today to make the most significant difference for the children and families we serve?

+ What seed might we plant together today that could grow into a stronger, more inclusive, and inspiring early childhood community?

Questions for Reflection on Strengths and Successes-staff meetings

+ What are your greatest strengths as an educator, and how do they contribute to the children's growth and learning?

+ What strengths do you see in our team, program, or classroom community?

+ What made a particular teaching moment, project, or interaction successful?

+ What would be the best possible outcome for the children, families, and educators involved in this situation?

+ What are the benefits of focusing on children's strengths and interests?

+ How do you see this approach affecting the children's development and the overall learning environment?

+ What has worked well before when addressing similar challenges or opportunities?

+ What past successes can we build upon to enhance our practices or program?

+ What opportunities do you see to enhance the children's learning experiences or our team's collaboration?

+ How could we mine the value of our diverse skills and perspectives to create something meaningful?

+ What steps can you take to bring this idea or vision to life?

+ How does this situation inspire you to try something new or think differently?

+ What created the passion or excitement for this idea, and how can we sustain it?

+ How could this practice, activity, or idea become more inclusive for all children and families?

+ How could we adapt this approach to have a more significant impact on our program or community?

Consider the following questions when creating staff meeting plans.

+ Is it formatted the same way every time?

+ Is it a top-down approach where the director leads the staff meeting by bringing up everything that is not working?

+ Their limited resources and lack of experience prevent them from exploring all possibilities.

+ Are people leaving with smiles on their faces?

+ Is Staff leaving looking drained?

Learning more about children at parent-teacher conferences

+ What do you see as your child's greatest strengths or talents?

+ What does your child enjoy doing the most at home or in their free time?

+ What are some qualities you love most about your child?

+ Can you share a time when you were proud of your child? What made it meaningful?

+ What has worked well in the past to support your child's learning or behavior?

+ What are your hopes and dreams for your child this school year and beyond?

+ If this school year is a booming success for your child, what would that look like to you?

+ Are there any areas where your child could grow or be challenged further?

+ What areas present opportunities for your child's growth and challenges?

+ Can you identify areas where your child could grow or be challenged further? What areas offer opportunities for your child's growth and challenges?

+ How can we, as a team, create opportunities for your child to thrive and feel confident?

+ What have you found to be the most effective ways to motivate or encourage your child at home?

+ How can I best support your child's learning and well-being in the classroom?

+ Would you like to share anything specific about your child's interests, needs, or preferences so that we can better support them?

+ What's one thing you'd like your child to take away from their experience this year?

+ If we could work on one big goal together for your child, what would you like that to be?

+ How can we ensure that our communication and partnership stay strong throughout the school year.

Appendix B

The TRF and all related content, including but not limited to accompanying graphics, templates, and training materials, are the intellectual property of Ellen M. Drolette.

You may reproduce templates as they are currently.

For permission requests, like co-constructing a new way of using the framework, licensing inquiries, or information on how to implement the TRF in your organization or training program, please contact:

Ellen M. Drolette

Positivespinllc.com

Positivespinllc@gmail.com

Triple R Individual Child Planning Template

Use this fillable template to the right to create a strengths-based plan for individual children using the TRF: Relevant, Relationship, and Reflect. This format supports developmentally appropriate, responsive, and connected planning tailored to each child's unique needs.

Child Profile

Name: _____

Date of Birth: _____Date of Plan:_____

Teacher/Team Members:_____

TRIPLE R	PLANNING QUESTIONS	YOUR NOTES
RELEVANT	What's meaningful or interesting to this child? How can I connect learning to their strengths, culture, or current experiences?	
RELATIONSHIP	How can I strengthen our connection? What strategies help this child feel safe, seen, and included?	
REFLECT	What do I notice about their behavior, communication, or learning patterns? How will I adjust based on what's working or not working?	

Triple R Lesson Planning Template for ECE

Use this fillable template to the right to design lesson plans rooted in the TRF: Relevant, Relationship, and Reflect. This approach ensures learning is meaningful, connection-centered, and reflective for both children and educators.

TRIPLE R	PLANNING QUESTIONS	YOUR PLAN
RELEVANT	What's meaningful to this group of children right now? How can I connect the lesson to their experiences, interests, or culture?	
RELATIONSHIP	How will this lesson build connection? What opportunities exist for collaboration, empathy, or co-regulation?	
REFLECT	Where can I build in time for reflection? How will I know what worked and what needs adjustment?	

Triple R Framework: A Printable Guide for Adult Learning Facilitators

RELEVANCE

Ask: "Why this? Why now?"

Use real-life challenges, current needs, and role-specific examples

Provide choice and autonomy in how learners engage with the content

RELATIONSHIP

Build safety and trust before content delivery

Use small groups, partner dialogue, co-facilitation

Invite personal voice and value lived experience

REFLECTION

Include prompts like: "What's already working?" or "What does this mean for my practice?"

Incorporate journaling, think-pair-share, or quiet pause time

Close with action steps or meaning-making

Appendix C

General Questions that can be used with the 5 D's

DEFINE the question: What are we seeking to understand?
+ What's the current challenge or opportunity before us?

+ How can we reword this question to be more positive and motivational?

+ Rather than asking "How can we repair ___?", try "How might we grow ___?"

DISCOVER: What's Already Working?
+ Recall a recent work experience that left you feeling energized or proud. What happened?

+ Which strengths did you or others use?

DREAM: Imagine the Best Possible Future
+ If we were thriving in this area, what would we see, hear, and feel?

+ What would a child or colleague say about our environment?

DESIGN: Let's Build on What Works
+ What are 1–2 small steps can we take this week to bring our dream closer?

+ What resources, relationships, or routines already exist to support this?

DELIVER / DESTINY: Make It Real, Make It Yours

+ What's one commitment I (or we) can make right now?

+ Who can I invite into this process with me?

Appendix D

Staff Meeting Template

Date:

Time:

Location:

Welcome and Warm-Up (10 minutes)

Opening Circle:
+ Begin the meeting with a brief mindfulness activity or gratitude exercise.

> Example: "Share one thing you're grateful for in your work this week."

Icebreaker Activity:
+ Incorporate a playful, team-building game such as:

> "Two Truths and a Wish" (the staff share two truths about their work this week and one wish for the future).

> A quick collaborative game like "Pass the Clap" or "One-Word Story" can energize the group.

Appreciative Check-In (15 minutes)
Positive Highlights:

+ Invite each team member to share a success or joyous moment they experienced recently. Example prompts:

> "What's one thing you did this week that made a difference for a child or family?"

> "What's a moment this week that made you smile?"

> Acknowledge team or individual achievements. Example: "Let's celebrate [staff member's name] for [specific accomplishment or action]."

Exploration and Reflection (20 minutes):

For longer staff meetings, break into table groups and have discussions.

+ Discussion

> What's working well in our classroom environments?

> What would it look like if we could create the ideal learning environment for children?

> What small steps can we take this month to get closer to our vision?

> How can we sustain and celebrate our progress?

+ Encourage collaborative brainstorming and note key ideas on a shared board or paper.

Playful Collaboration (15 minutes)

Interactive Activity:

Engage in a creative or playful task to reinforce teamwork and problem-solving.

Examples:

> Build a classroom strategy using LEGO or blocks ("What does a thriving team look like?").

> Role-play a challenging scenario and collaboratively problem-solve in a fun, low-pressure way.

Discuss insights or takeaways from the activity.

Action Steps and Commitments (10 minutes)

Set Goals:
Summarize key takeaways and establish action steps.

+ Example: "What's one thing we can each commit to trying or improving before our next meeting?"

Assign Follow-Ups:
Outline who will take responsibility for specific tasks or initiatives discussed.

Closing Reflection and Gratitude (10 minutes)
End with a reflective question to inspire positivity and forward thinking. Example: What's one thing you're looking forward to in the coming week?"

Express gratitude for the team's hard work and contributions. End with a positive, playful note, such as a joke, a team cheer, or a fun chant.

Optional
Provide snacks, coffee, or small tokens of appreciation to make the meeting feel exceptional and supportive.

Appendix E

For Early Childhood Programs

Program Name:

Date:

Vision Statement

Purpose: The vision statement reflects your program's long-term aspirations and what you hope to achieve for children, families, and the community.

Prompts to Guide Development:

What is the ultimate goal of our program?

How do we envision the children in our care thriving in the future?

What lasting impact do we want to have on families and the community?

Brainstorm Space:

Write key phrases or ideas shared by staff, families, and stakeholders.

Refine into a clear, inspiring vision statement.

Philosophy Statement

Purpose: The philosophy statement outlines the beliefs and principles guiding your early childhood education approach.

Prompts to Guide Development:

+ What is our belief about how children learn and grow?

+ What role do families, educators, and the community play in supporting children?

+ How do we define success in early childhood education?

Brainstorm Space:

> Note specific beliefs about child development, family engagement, and teaching practices.

> Highlight keywords or phrases that resonate and refine them into a cohesive statement.

Stakeholder Input and Feedback

+ Engage staff, families, and community members to gather feedback on the draft statements.

+ Ask guiding questions:

> Does this reflect the core values of our program?

> Do these statements inspire and resonate with you?

> Are there any key elements we are missing?

Feedback Notes:

Mission Statement

Purpose: The mission statement defines the purpose of your program, focusing on what you do daily to achieve your vision.

Prompts to Guide Development:

+ What is our core purpose as an early childhood program?

+ What do we do to support children, families, and staff?

+ What values guide our work?

Brainstorm Space:
+ List daily practices, core services, and values.

+ Refine into a concise, actionable mission statement.

Final Review and Approval
+ Share revised statements with leadership or governance teams for final input.

+ Approve and publish the finalized vision, mission, and philosophy statements.

Implementation Plan

Communicate the statements to all stakeholders (staff, families, and community).

Incorporate the vision, mission, and philosophy into:
> Staff training and onboarding.

> Marketing materials and program communications.

> Daily practices, curriculum planning, and decision-making processes.

Signatures
Program Director:

_____

Date: _____

Board Chair (if applicable):

_____

Date: _____

APPENDIX F

Activities to Guide the Development of Vision, Mission, and Philosophy

Values Exploration Activity:

+ Provide participants with core values (e.g., respect, inclusion, play, equity).

+ Ask each person to identify their top five values.

+ Discuss common themes and integrate these into the statements.

Vision Mapping:

+ Create a collaborative "vision board" using images, words, and drawings representing the program's future impact.

+ Use the vision board as inspiration to draft a clear, concise vision statement.

Mission Brainstorming Sessions:

+ Use prompts like:

> What do we want children to experience daily in our program?

> How do we support families and the community?

> What makes our program unique?

+ Consolidate responses into key themes to build the mission statement.

Philosophy-Reflection Circle:

+ Discuss key questions as a team:

> How do we believe children learn best?

> What role do families and educators play in a child's success?

> What practices align with our values and goals?

> Write individual reflections, then refine a shared philosophy together.

Stakeholder Surveys:

+ Invite input from families, community partners, and staff through surveys with open-ended questions about the program's strengths and aspirations.

+ Use the data to inform the statements and ensure they reflect the community's perspective.

Draft and Feedback Rounds:

+ Create draft statements and present them to stakeholders for feedback.

+ Use questions like:

> Does this reflect our shared goals and values?

> Is this inspiring and clear?

> What adjustments would make it more meaningful?

Staff Interview protocol with a strengths-based lens

Introduction
Start by explaining the interview process to the candidate, setting the tone that the conversation will be centered on their strength and how these have helped them succeed.

Example:

"In this interview, we will focus on the strengths you bring to the workplace. I'll ask about your experiences and how you've used your natural strengths to succeed in various situations. The goal is to learn more about what energizes and motivates you and how those qualities align with the role we are offering."

Warm-Up Questions
These questions help the candidate feel comfortable and provide a foundation for discussing their strengths.

+ What is your background and experience?

+ What are you most proud of in your career so far?

+ What aspects of your current or previous roles do you enjoy the most?

Exploration
Dive into specific strengths by asking open-ended questions and encouraging the candidate to reflect on experiences.

Sample Questions:

+ What do you consider being your most significant strengths? Can you share an example of a time when you used that strength to solve a problem or achieve a goal?

+ Tell me about when you felt energized or motivated at work. W.hat were you doing, and how did your strengths contribute to that experience?

+ What role do you gravitate toward when working with a team? How does your natural strength support that role?

+ Have you ever faced a challenge at work that required you to use your strengths in new or unexpected ways? How did you handle it?

+ Tell me about when you received positive feedback from a colleague or supervisor. What do you think they were recognizing in you?

Action

Explore how the candidate uses their strengths to meet the demands of a job or workplace environment. This helps you gauge their fit for the role and whether their strengths align with your organization's needs.

Sample Questions:

+ Can you explain how you've used your strengths to contribute to a successful team effort?

+ How do you leverage your strengths to stay focused and productive in a stressful environment? Can you share an example?

+ We value creativity and innovation. How have you used your strengths to bring fresh ideas to the table in past positions?

Development

How does the candidate continue to build on their strengths and grow?

Sample Questions:

+ What steps do you take to build on your strengths and improve your work?

+ Are there any new strengths you'd like to develop in your next role? How do you plan to do that?

+ How do you receive and respond to feedback about your strengths or areas for growth?

Closing Questions

Sample Questions

+ Based on our conversation, how will your strengths help you succeed in this role?

+ What's one thing you're most excited to bring to the team, based on your strengths?

+ Is there anything else you'd like to share about how your strengths align with this position?

How can we get more early childhood programs to adopt this initiative?
+ Highlight each child's individual talents and abilities. This boosts self-esteem and encourages a love of learning.

+ Children who believe in their ability to improve are motivated to learn from their mistakes and build resilience.

+ Helping children name and recognize their emotions fosters self-awareness.

+ Daily activities build cooperation, empathy, and social connections.

+ Warm, supportive teacher-child relationships create a safe and trusting learning environment crucial for both academic and emotional development.

+ Inclusive environments that celebrate diversity and individual strengths make children feel valued and included. A sense of belonging is fostered among children in environments that embrace diversity and individual talents.

+ Focus and calmness in young children can be fostered through simple breathing exercises or sensory activities.

+ Gratitude exercises cultivate optimism and positive emotions in children.

+ Positive education naturally fosters children's problem-solving skills, creativity, and resilience.

+ Children use pretend play to learn about social situations, build empathy, and overcome challenges.

+ Educator burnout can be lessened through reflective practices, mindfulness, and supportive professional networks.

+ Appreciative Inquiry-based staff development, incorporating strengths-based reflection, promotes a collaborative and supportive work environment for educators.

+ Children's emotional development is key to their future mental well-being.

+ Prioritizing well-being boosts cognitive skills, focus, and a passion for learning.

+ Stronger connections with educators and peers promote positive social behavior and reduce behavioral challenges.

Guide for Consultancy with an Appreciative Flair: A Strengths-Based Model

This model invites Early Childhood Educators (ECEs) to engage in deep reflection, creative dreaming, and strengths-based planning through a supportive, appreciative process. The goal is to move from challenge to possibility with empathy, curiosity, and optimism.

Step 1: Setting the Stage

Create a safe, welcoming environment. The speaker (ECE) briefly shares a current challenge or situation they would like support around.

Guiding Prompt:

"What's something on your mind that you'd like to explore together today?"

Step 2: Strengths Spotting

Before diving into the challenge, the note-taker reflects on strengths they observe in the speaker's story, words, or energy.

Guiding Prompt:

"What strengths are already present in this story?"

+ This helps reframe the conversation with a foundation of capability and resilience.

Step 3: Reframing with Intention

We invite the speaker to reframe the challenge into a vision of what they want more of.

Guiding Prompts:

+ "How do you want to feel in this situation?"

+ "What would you see, hear, and experience if things were going well?"

+ "What is the positive opposite of the current struggle?"

+ Encourage descriptive, sensory-rich responses. Paint the picture completely.

Step 4: Deep Listening

The note-taker listens and writes. No advice or comments yet—just presence and curiosity.

Guiding Principle:

"Listen with your whole heart. Capture words, emotions, images, and strengths."

Step 5: Appreciative Inquiry & Gentle Curiosity

After the speaker finishes, the notetaker may share what stood out, using reflective language, metaphors, or imagery. Ask clarifying or expanding questions.

Sample Questions:

+ "Can you tell me more about that moment you described?"

+ "What would success feel like in your body?"

+ "If this vision came to life, what would be different for you or your team?"

Step 6: Stillness & Resonance

Take a few moments of quiet. Let the ideas settle.

Guiding Prompt:

"What is resonating most deeply for you right now?"

+ This allows space for internal clarity before action planning.

Step 7: Dream and Design

Together, co-create possibilities. What might be one small step forward?

What could this look like if nothing stood in the way?

Guiding Prompts:

+ "What would your ideal outcome be?"

+ "If you could wave a magic wand, what would happen next?"

+ "What is one bold or beautiful step you could try?"

Use a strengths-based lens: What assets do you already have to support this dream?

Step 8: Reflection and Journaling
End with quiet reflection and a journal prompt.

Guiding Prompts:

+ "What assets did I discover in myself today?"

+ "What am I learning about my strengths or approach?"

+ "How am I feeling on a scale of 1–10 (1 = best, 10 = worst)?"

+ "What will I take with me from this process?"

Close the session with gratitude and affirmation of the speaker's growth and insight.

Appendix G

Template for working with consultancy

Consultancy with an Appreciative Flair

A Strengths-Based Reflection and Planning Template

Speaker Name:

_____

Note-taker Name:

_____

Date: _____

Step 1: Set the Stage
What challenge or situation would you like to explore today?

(Speaker shares briefly)

Step 2: Strengths Spotting
What strengths are already visible in this situation?

(Note-taker reflects observed strengths)

Step 3: Reframing with Intention

As the speaker, describe your vision for what you want more of:

How do you want to feel?

What do you want to see?

What do you want to hear?

What is the positive opposite of your challenge?

Step 4: Deep Listening

(Note taker listens quietly and writes notes. No comments during this step.)

Notes:

Step 5: Reflective Questions and Insights

(Note taker shares metaphors, reflections, and gently asks for more detail.)

What stood out in what you heard?

What questions or images came to mind?

Step 6: Stillness and Resonance

Take a few moments of silence.

What is resonating with you right now?

Step 7: Dream and Design

Co-create a vision or plan. Think bravely.

What's one possibility or idea that excites you?

What is one small step forward?

What strengths will help you move in this direction?

Step 8: Reflection and Journaling

What assets have I discovered in myself today?

What have I learned about myself or my situation?

On a scale of 1–10, how am I feeling now? (1 = best, 10 = worst)

Final reflection on this process:

APPENDIX **H**

Book Club Guide & Reflection Prompts

Welcome to Your Book Club Guide:

More Than We Imagined was written to spark not just reflection, but conversation and practical change. Whether you're reading this on your own, discussing it with colleagues, or bringing it to a community of practice, this guide is here to help you go deeper.

Each chapter comes with thoughtful discussion questions and reflection ideas designed to:

+ Invite honest dialogue.

+ Connect big ideas to daily practice.

+ Make space for personal insight and shared discovery.

There's no right or wrong way to use this guide. Some groups tackle one chapter per session; others pick the questions that feel most meaningful. You can respond aloud, journal, or use the prompts as conversation starters in staff meetings or family child care gatherings.

May these questions help you uncover even more than you imagined, in yourself, in each other, and in every setting that matters.

Before each session:

+ Read the chapter.

+ Highlight a line or idea that resonates.

+ Reflect on how it connects to your work and life.

During discussion:

+ Take turns sharing reflections.

+ Listen with curiosity; no fixing, no judging.

+ Use the Reflection Ideas as journal prompt or quiet pauses during your gathering.

Afterward:

+ Choose one insight or action step to carry forward until you meet again.

+ Celebrate what you're doing well and keep asking appreciative questions.

When we explore what's working, what lifts us up, and what we believe is possible, we shape more than we imagined. Thank you for being part of this journey.

Chapter 1: Start Where You Are

Questions:

What does "start where you are" mean to you in your current role?

Can you think of a moment when accepting where you were helped you move forward?

What does "meeting others where they are" look like in practice?

Reflection Idea:

Write about one area of your work or life where you wish you were "further along." How might starting exactly where you are unlock new possibilities?

Chapter 2: Curiosity as a Catalyst
Questions:

How has curiosity helped you find solutions in situations?

When do you feel most curious about your work or personal life?

What is one curious question you want to practice asking more often?

Reflection Idea:

Keep a "Curiosity Journal" for one week. Jot down curious questions you ask (or wish you'd asked) and what they opened up for you or others.

Chapter 3: The Triple R Framework (TRF)
Questions:

Which of the three R's (Relevance, Relationships, Reflection) feels strongest for you right now? Which needs more attention?

How can the TRF guide your daily interactions with children, families, or colleagues?

What is one small shift you can make this week to bring the TRF to life?

Reflection Idea:

Sketch or map out your week ahead. Mark one moment where you will intentionally build relevance, one for relationships, and one for reflection.

Chapter 4: Priorities with Purpose
Questions:

What is most important to you in your work with children and families?

How do you keep your daily tasks aligned with your deeper purpose?

Where might you need to pause and realign your priorities right now?

Reflection Idea:

Make a "Not-To-Do List," write one task or habit that no longer serves your purpose, and decide how to let it go or adjust it.

Chapter 5: The Strengths Shift
Questions:

How would you explain "the strengths shift" in your own words?

Whose strengths have you overlooked and how could you see them differently?

How does focusing on strengths change the way you feel about your work?

Reflection Idea:

Write a short "Strengths Note" to yourself, a child, or a colleague, highlight one genuine strength and how it shows up in daily life.

Chapter 6: The Architecture of Possibility
Questions:

What does "architecture of possibility" mean to you?

Can you share a time when someone created possibilities for you?

How can you help design spaces or conversations that make more possible for others?

Reflection Idea:

Draw or list three "possibility doors" you could open for someone else this month. What's one step to open the first door?

Chapter 7: What Lifts Us Up?

Questions:

What lifts you up on a hard day?

How do you notice and nurture what lifts your team, children, or families?

How might your program celebrate small wins?

Reflection Idea:

Create a "Lift Me Up" list, include small actions, people, or places you can turn to when you need to recharge.

Chapter 8: Strengths at the Center

Questions:

What does it look like to put strengths at the center of your relationships or teaching?

How can you involve children and families in spotting strengths??

What might impede keeping strengths at the center and how can you address it?

Reflection Idea:

Choose a child, colleague, or family you interact with regularly. For one week, look for three strengths in them each day. Record what you notice.

Chapter 9: Infusing Strengths Into Everyday Practice

Questions:

What is one daily routine that could benefit from a strengths-based approach?

How can you share strengths-based observations with families?

What helps you remember to see the strengths when things feel hard?

Reflection Idea:

Pick a challenging routine or transition time. Journal a strengths-based script or plan for how you might handle it differently this week.

Chapter 10: What We Believe Shapes What We Do

Joseph's Story (Simultaneity Principle – "The Questions That Changed the Story")

+ What stories from your childhood do you now see differently after gaining new perspective?

+ Can you think of a time when someone asked you a question that changed how you saw a situation or yourself?

+ What do you notice about how your emotions shape your memories?

+ How might we ask questions that open up, not shut down conversation and understanding with others?

+ How can acknowledging multiple perspectives help us build stronger relationships with children, families, or colleagues?

The Constructionist Story (Constructionist Principle – "From Assumptions to Understanding")

+ Reflect on a time when your assumptions about best practice shifted. What sparked the change?

+ What messages are your program's walls, words, and rituals sending to children and families?

+ How does the way you talk about children shape how others see them and how they see themselves?

+ What inherited practices have you questioned, and what new ones have you created?

+ In what ways can we co-create our program culture with children, families, and co-workers?

Praxis Story (Anticipatory Principle – "Rewriting the Narrative")
+ What self-fulfilling prophecies have you carried and are they still serving you?

+ When have you surprised yourself by achieving something you thought was beyond your reach?

+ How do you speak to yourself when you're working toward a difficult goal?

+ What future vision do you hold for yourself and what actions can you take today to move toward it?

+ How might you support children or colleagues in building more positive internal narratives?

Marathon Story (Poetic Principle – "Running Within")
+ What story did you once tell yourself about who you were and how has that changed?

+ What details or small moments have shaped your biggest personal transformations?

+ How can you reframe everyday moments (like a classroom transition or a staff meeting) as meaningful?

+ What traditions or rituals help you reconnect to your values?

+ If you rewrote your narrative today, what strengths and values would take center stage?

Positive Principle Story (Positive Principle – "The Strengths They Carried")

+ When have you seen a strengths-based approach transform a challenge into an opportunity?

+ What happens when you focus on what's working rather than what's broken?

+ Think of someone you've supported—what strengths did you notice and amplify?

+ How can we help others see their own value when systems or language have told them otherwise?

+ What positive questions could you bring to your next challenge or meeting?

Chapter 11 Start with Humanity: Living the Questions

+ What assumptions were being made about Patrick, and how did the teacher's decision to pause and observe shift the narrative?

+ How might the story have unfolded differently if the teacher had responded with correction instead of curiosity?

+ What does it mean to "start with humanity" in early childhood settings and what gets in the way of doing that consistently?

+ Think of a child you've worked with who challenged you. What questions might you ask now to better understand their experience?

+ How does this story invite us to reflect on the difference between "fixing a behavior" and "seeing a child"?

REFERENCES

AI Commons. (n.d.). Appreciative Inquiry - A Brief History - The Appreciative Inquiry Commons. The Appreciative Inquiry Commons. Retrieved December 22, 2024, from https://aicommons.champlain.edu/learn/appreciative-inquiry-brief-history/

Alliance for Early Success. (n.d.). Historic State investment in Child Care. Alliance For Early Success. https://earlysuccess.org/vermont-historic-child-care-investment

Asana. (2024, March 1). How To Write a Vision Statement: Steps & Examples [2024] • Asana. Asana. Retrieved November 21, 2024, from https://asana.com/resources/vision-statement

Bhandri, S. (2024, February 25th). What is the 'Us vs Them' mentality? WebMD. Retrieved March 01, 2025, from https://www.webmd.com/mental-health/what-is-the-us-against-them-mentality

Brightwheel.blog. (2023, February 17). How to Use Open-Ended Questions with Preschoolers (with 50+ Examples). Brightwheel. Retrieved January 21, 2025, from https://mybrightwheel.com/blog/open-ended-questions-for-preschoolers

Campbell, A. B. (2025, 23 January). Community and Identity: Engaging Children in Conversation with Dr. Patrick Makokoro [Podcast]. In Voice of Your Village (#320 ed.) [Podcast]. Seed and Sew. https://www.seedandsew.org/voices-of-your-village

Campbell, A. B., & Stauble, L. E. (2023). Tiny Humans, Big Emotions: How to Navigate Tantrums, Meltdowns, and Defiance to Raise Emotionally Intelligent Children. HarperCollins Publishers. pg. 13

Cooperrider, D. L., & Stavros, J. M. (2015). Appreciative Inquiry Handbook: For leaders of change (2nd edition, revised. (2nd ed.). Crown Custon Publishing.

Cooperrider, D. L., & Whitney, D. (2005). Appreciative Inquiry: A Positive Revolution in Change. Berrett-Koehler Publishers.

Emamzadeh, A. (2019, August 9). The Psychology of Us Vs. Them. Psychology Today. Retrieved February 7, 2025, from https://www.psychologytoday.com/us/blog/finding-new-home/201908/the-psychology-us-vs-them

Emmons, R. (2017, October 11). Three Surprising Ways That Gratitude Works at Work. Greater Good Science Center. Retrieved January 9, 2025, from https://greatergood.berkeley.edu/article/item/three_surprising_ways_that_gratitude_works_at_work

Frothingham, M. B. (2024, January 29). Emotional Intelligence (EQ): Components and Examples. Simply Psychology. Retrieved January 19, 2025, from https://www.simplypsychology.org/emotional-intelligence.html

Goffin, S. (2015). Professionalizing Early Childhood Education as a Field of Practice: A Guide to the Next Era. Redleaf Press.

Gross, S. (2024, April 1). Playmaker News - TEDx. Life is Good. Retrieved January 14, 2025, from https://www.lifeisgood.com/playmakerproject/TEDx-2023.html

Heckman, J. (2023, 01 January). ROI Research Toolkid. Heckman: the economics of Human Potential. Retrieved January 13, 2025, from https://heckmanequation.org/resource/13-roi-toolbox/

The International Positive Education Network. (2025, 0 0). About Us. IPEN-Network. Retrieved 27 09, 2025, from https://ipen-network.com/about-us/

Kelm, J. B. (2014). The Joy of Appreciative Living: Your 28-Day Plan to Greater Happiness Using the Principles of Appreciative Inquiry. Venet Publishing.

Life is Good Playmaker Project. (2025, January 1). Life is Good Playmaker Project. Life is Good Playmaker Project. https://www.lifeisgood.com/playmakerproject/playmaker-about.html

Lynch, J., & Scott, W. (1999). Running Within. Human Kinetics. p. 52

Lyubomirsky, S. (2007, January 1). The how of happiness: A scientific approach to getting the life you want. Psycnet. Retrieved January 31, 2025, from https://psycnet.apa.org/record/2008-05086-000

Merchen, A., & Richards, A. (2024, October 4). How Vermont's Act 76 Revolutionizes Child Care Funding. U.S. Chamber Foundation. Retrieved February 4, 2025, from https://www.uschamberfoundation.org/education/how-vermonts-act-76-revolutionizes-child-care-funding?

Mohr, B. J., & Magruder Watkins, J. (n.d.). The Essentials of Appreciative Inquiry: A Roadmap for Creating Positive Futures. Pegasus Communication, 3. pg. 3

NAEYC. (n.d.). Power to the Profession. Power to the Profession. Retrieved 01, 2025, from https://powertotheprofession.org/source-documents/

Neuro Launch Editorial Staff. (2025, January 28th). What is a Pollyanna Personality. Neuro launch. Retrieved March March 16th, 2025, 2025, from https://neurolaunch.com/what-is-a-pollyanna-personality/

Noren, A. (2011, August 10). Measuring Gratitude. Gratitude Works. Retrieved January 8, 2025, from https://emmons.faculty.ucdavis.edu/measuring-gratitude/

R, P., M.F., S., Bergeman, C.S., Pedersen, N.L., Nesselroade, J. z., & McClearn, G.E. (1992, August 1). Optimism, pessimism and mental health: A twin/adoption analysis. Science Direct. Retrieved January 31, 2025, from https://www.sciencedirect.com/science/article/abs/pii/019188699290009E

Seligman, M. E.P. (2006). Learned Optimism: How to Change Your Mind and Your Life. Knopf Doubleday Publishing Group.

September 1980 , pp. 469. (1980, September). Behavioral and Brain Sciences, Volume 3(issue 3), 469. https://doi.org/10.1017/S0140525X00006166

Stavros, J. M., & Torres, C. (2018). Conversations Worth Having: Using Appreciative Inquiry to Fuel Productive and Meaningful Engagement. Berrett-Koehler Publishers, Incorporated. pg. 30

Stiller, R. (2024). Bette rand Better: Creating a Culture of Purpose, Excellence, and Transformative Human Engagement (1st ed.). McGraw Hill.

Taylor, S. E., Kemeny, M. E., Reed, G. M., Bower, J. E., & Gruenewald, T. L. (2004). Psychological resources, positive illusions, and health. American Psychologist, 55(1), 99-109. https://www.researchgate.net/profile/Margaret-Kemeny/publication/11946309_Psychological_resources_positive_illusions_and_health/links/00b4951c96f6febb5f000000/Psychological-Resources-Positive-Illusions-and-Health.pdf

Titterton, S. (2019, June 1). Early Childhood Education in Vermont Advancing as a Profession: A Workforce Engagement Project. VTAEYC. Retrieved January 31, 2025, from https://www.vtaeyc.org/wp-content/uploads/2019/09/ECE-as-Prof_REPORT-Final.pdf

Toxic Positivity. (n.d.). https://www.psychologytoday.com/us/basics/toxic-positivity. https://www.psychologytoday.com/us/basics/toxic-positivity

USA Today. (2025, January 23). Ilona Maher doesn't have imposter syndrome: 'It's OK to be proud.' See viral clip. MSN.com. Retrieved January 25, 2025, from https://www.msn.com/en-us/entertainment/celebrities/ilona-maher-doesn-t-have-imposter-syndrome-it-s-ok-to-be-proud-see-viral-clip/ar-AA1xJCM1

Vermont Department of Children and Families. (2024, October 7). More Vermont Families Qualify for Child Care Financial Assistance. https://dcf.vermont.gov/. Retrieved February 4, 2025, from https://dcf.vermont.gov/dcf-news/more-vermont-families-qualify-child-care-financial-assistance

Vogt, E., Brown, J., & Issacs, D. (2024, July 7th). The Art of Powerful Questions. https://www.sparc.bc.ca/wp-content/uploads/2020/11/the-art-of-powerful-questions.pdf

Washington, V. (2019). Valora Washington Keynote (transcript) [University of Washington] [Keynote]. washington.edu. https://depts.washington.edu/eedu/LDRS/transcripts/L01-ValoraKeynote.html

Whitney, D. K., Trosten-Bloom, A., Cooperrider, D., & Kaplan, B. S. (2013). Encyclopedia of Positive Questions: Using Appreciative Inquiry to Bring Out the Best in Your Organization (2nd ed.). Crown Custom Publishing. pg. 10

World Forum Foundation. (2025, Jaunary 1). World Forum Foundation. World Forum Foundation. https://worldforumfoundation.org/about-us/

Yilmaz, E. (2024, December 28). Self-Fulfilling Prophecy: Definition, Examples, & Theories. Berkley Wellbeing. Burkleywellbeing.com

Zhao, B., & Luengo-Prado, M. J. (2024, October 21). Recent Trends in Vermont Childcare: A Decrease in Capacity, Increases in Cost and Quality, and Policy Responses. Bostonfed.org. Retrieved February 4, 2025, from https://www.bostonfed.org/publications/new-england-public-policy-center-regional-briefs/2024/recent-trends-in-vermont-childcare.aspx

www.ingramcontent.com/pod-product-compliance
Lightning Source LLC
Chambersburg PA
CBHW061742120626
46550CB00005B/1864